H. STUART HUGHES

Oswald Spengler

A CRITICAL ESTIMATE

REVISED EDITION

CHARLES SCRIBNER'S SONS, NEW YORK

Printed in the United States of America

For

SUZANNE

ACKNOWLEDGMENTS

I am indebted to the Institute for Advanced Study, Princeton, N. J., under whose auspices I did the research for this book; to the editors of *Die Welt als Geschichte,* Professors Hans Erich Stier and Fritz Ernst, who helped me with advice and information; to Spengler's niece and literary executor, Dr. Hildegard Kornhardt, who generously supplied me with biographical data nowhere else available; and above all to Professors Crane Brinton and Felix Gilbert, who read and criticized the entire manuscript. For the paperback edition (1962), I have restricted myself to making a minimum of verbal corrections in the text, inserting half a dozen new footnotes, expanding the bibliography to take account of recently-published literature, and adding two explanatory appendices.

CONTENTS

CHAPTER ONE

1918 : A PORTENT

IN THE summer of 1918, only a few months before the final defeat of the German Empire in the First World War, there began to appear in the bookstores of Germany and Austria a heavy volume, by a totally unknown scholar called Oswald Spengler, bearing the provocative title *Der Untergang des Abendlandes*—the decline of the West. After a few weeks of public hesitation, the book started to sell, and it has continued to sell ever since. In Germany, it soon became the center of the most excited and bitter literary controversy of the post-war years. Abroad, it won the admiration of the half-educated and the scorn of the judicious. In attenuated form, the controversy has continued to the present date—and has recently shown signs of a rather unexpected vitality.

Since the original appearance of Spengler's portentous work, the scholarly world—and more particularly the historical profession—has been embarrassed to know what to do about it. Although based on an impressive amount of reading, *The Decline of the West* is obviously not a respectable performance from the standpoint of scholarship. It is too metaphysical, too dogmatic—in all respects, too extreme. Yet there it sits—a massive stumbling-block in the path of true knowledge. In their efforts to dispose of it, the scholars have resorted to a variety of tactics: bitter invective, icy scorn, urbane mockery, or simply pretending that it is not there. Again and again they have warned their students, and through them, the public, against so dangerous a

1

piece of literature. Yet the public has refused to be warned. Through three decades, the young and the non-professional have blithely continued to buy Spengler, to read him (perhaps skipping the more difficult chapters), and to find in him a source of profound intellectual excitement.

It is perhaps owing to this split in attitude between the learned world and the public that the existing literature on Spengler falls into two distinct classes. By far the larger portion consists of scholarly analyses, almost invariably critical in tone, of specific aspects of the *Decline* or of Spengler's later writings. The rest can be described as the work of enthusiasts—inexact, impressionistic, and frequently naive. Between these two, there is practically nothing. The present volume represents an effort to fill this gap. It is intended both for the scholarly world and for the general public. It will endeavor to analyze the criticisms of the former and to explain the enthusiasm of the latter—and, if possible, to offer a basis for their reconciliation. Such a basis can be found only by viewing Spengler's work in the broadest possible perspective—as a manifestation of the enormous effort of intellectual re-evaluation that has characterized our century. That century, of which Spengler felt himself to be the prophet, has now reached its half-way point. Sufficient time has passed to permit us to see Spengler in proper relation to his contemporaries and successors who faced similar intellectual problems. Although several of them were far greater than he in the depth and rigor of their analysis, none was so bold and self-confident in charting the course of the century opening before him. In this respect also, the passage of time has permitted us to make a judgment: with fifty years of history behind us, with the rise of totalitarianism, the advent of mass culture, the experience of two world wars and the prospect of a third, we are at length in a position to evaluate Spengler as political controversialist, as prophet, and as diagnostician of our time.

*   *   *

In the preface to the first edition of the *Decline,* Spengler declared that the First World War "was an element in the prem-

isses from which the new world-picture could be made precise."
He added the wish—omitted without explanation from the English
translation—that his book "might not be entirely unworthy to
take its place beside the military achievements of Germany." [1]
Aside from these two statements, the war had practically nothing
to do with *The Decline of the West* except to delay its publication.

It was its author's first venture into the field of historical
writing. Although a man of university education with a doctor's
degree from Halle, Oswald Spengler was in no sense a recognized
representative of the German academic profession. A north German, the son of parents of a modest but respectable position in
life, Spengler was born in 1880 at Blankenburg, in the Harz
mountains. On his father's side he came from a line of mining
technicians, who had originally migrated to the Harz from South
Germany in the seventeenth century. Against his will and only
because of the steady decline of the Harz mines, Oswald's father
had given up the family profession and become a postal official.
To this paternal inheritance, according to Spengler's friend and
propagandist August Albers, the author of the *Decline* owed his
mathematical and scientific talents. His mother's family provided
the artistic bent. The maternal grandfather had been a *maître de
ballet,* and an aunt had been a well-known dancer. On both
sides, the family was Protestant, except for Spengler's grand-
mother, who was a Catholic from Munich. [2]

Oswald was the only surviving son, with three younger
sisters. The oldest of them, a talented painter, to whom her

[1] Oswald Spengler, *Der Untergang des Abendlandes: Umrisse einer Mor-
phologie der Weltgeschichte;* I: *Gestalt und Wirklichkeit* (Munich, 1923); II:
Welthistorische Perspektiven (Munich, 1922). Translated by Charles Francis
Atkinson as *The Decline of the West;* I: *Form and Actuality* (New York, 1926);
II: *Perspectives of World-History* (New York, 1928)—I, xv (all references are
to the English translation).

[2] The best published biographical account is by August Albers: "Oswald
Spengler," *Preussische Jahrbücher,* CLXXXII, 2. Heft, May 1923, pp. 129–
137; other biographical details are based on three letters to the author from
Spengler's niece, Dr. Hildegard Kornhardt, who is the editor of her uncle's posthumously-published writings.

brother was much attached, committed suicide in 1917, at the age of thirty-five. Soon after Oswald's birth, his parents moved to Halle, a change that seems to have meant a considerable improvement in the family's financial position. At least we know that they were able to provide their son with a university education—and in Germany such an education has traditionally been attainable only by those of more than average means. After his graduation from a classical high school in Halle, Spengler followed the customary German practice of attending two or three universities in turn: Munich, Berlin, and finally Halle, where he returned to complete his doctor's thesis. His major subjects of study were mathematics and the natural sciences. Meanwhile he had upheld another tradition by making several trips to Italy, which the august example of Goethe had established as the goal of the young German's cultural pilgrimage. And he had shown characteristic temerity in his choice of a thesis topic—the fragmentary writings of Heraclitus, long known as the most abstruse of the pre-Socratic philosophers.

In the autumn of 1903, with his thesis completed, Spengler presented himself for his oral examination. He failed the first time, then passed six months later. There followed the state examination for the teaching career, for which Spengler presented, in addition to his thesis subject, as a special theme, "The Development of the Organ of Sight in the Chief Stages of Animal Life"—a prelude to a long interest in the philosophical aspects of light and vision. His first teaching position was in Saarbrücken; he subsequently taught in Düsseldorf and Hamburg, and in 1908 he moved up a grade with an appointment to a Hamburg *Realgymnasium* or practical high school. Here, since the school was new and had as yet only a small faculty, he taught German, history, and geography in addition to his regular subjects. Evidently he was a good teacher. Former students have recalled that his lecture style was both lively and "intuitive"—a prophetic adjective—and (again a foretaste of the future) that he was already attacking the reigning cult of Darwinism. Although not given to harsh penalties, he maintained firm discipline in his classes. Personally, he led a withdrawn life. Yet he had apparently won the esteem of his colleagues, for both faculty and students were sorry to see him go when in 1910 he obtained a year's leave of absence.

Spengler never returned to teaching. Originally he had intended to stay in Hamburg, but finding that the climate aggravated the severe headaches from which he frequently suffered, he moved in 1911 to Munich. After his leave was over, he resigned his teaching position, and remained in Munich as a private scholar. Here he lived modestly on a small income, an inheritance from his mother, who had died in 1910. He supplemented it by writing reviews and short articles. With the outbreak of the First World War, however, Spengler fell into serious financial difficulties. Since he suffered from both a heart condition and acute nearsightedness, he was never called up for military service. But the greater part of his funds, which were in foreign securities, no longer brought in any interest. During the war years, Spengler lodged in a dreary slum, took his meals in cheap working-class restaurants, and wrote much of the *Decline* by candle-light. As a bachelor and city-dweller, he found it difficult to obtain even the bare necessities of food, heat, and clothing. He was sustained by the conviction that a great, inchoate idea was germinating inside him and that he must fight his way through the laborious process of bringing it to expression.

When he originally requested leave from teaching, he had no clear notion of what he was going to do. Apparently, he simply felt that he needed time to read, to write, and to think. In Munich, he read voraciously in the fields of history—including art history —and philosophy. He also continued the experiments in creative writing that he had begun during his Hamburg days. These efforts, we are told, included poems, dramas, and stories. Only one of them reached completion, a "sketch" entitled *Der Sieger* (The Victor) dating from 1910. It tells the story of a frail Japanese artist, drafted into military service for the war with Russia, who meets his death at the battle of Liaoyang. Shot down in a charge on an enemy battery, the artist, mortally wounded, draws with his own blood a picture of a Russian artillery officer confronting

him. The drawing represents his own personal victory, which at
the same time forms part of the greater victory of his country. In
this early sketch Spengler's literary talents appear to only medi-
ocre advantage: the style is over-colored and cluttered with ad-
jectives, the tone is extravagant and unsophisticated. Yet as a
psychological point of departure it is not without interest. It reveals its author as a nationalist and an apologist for military
glory who at the same time feels himself to be an artist. In the
symbolic act of drawing the Russian officer's picture, the two tendencies strive for reconciliation. But their union strikes us as
somewhat artificial—the product of a literary trick. The materials
for inner conflict are already apparent.[3]

*   *   *

Sometime in 1911, during his first year in Munich, the idea
for Spengler's ambitious work suddenly came to him. He himself
has related how the outbreak of the Second Moroccan Crisis—
which brought the German Empire and the French Republic
perilously close to armed conflict—opened his eyes to the true
nature of his own epoch:

> At that time the World-War appeared to me both as immi-
> nent and also as the inevitable outward manifestation of the
> historical crisis, and my endeavour was to comprehend it from
> an examination of the spirit of the preceding centuries—not
> years . . . .
>   Thereafter I saw the present—the approaching World-
> War—in a quite other light. It was no longer a momentary
> constellation of casual facts due to national sentiments, per-
> sonal influences, or economic tendencies endowed with an
> appearance of unity and necessity by some historian's
> scheme of political or social cause-and-effect, but the type of
> *a historical change of phase* occurring within a great histor-
> ical organism of definable compass at the point preordained
> for it hundreds of years ago.[4]

[3] "Der Sieger" is included in Spengler's posthumously-published *Reden und
Aufsätze* (Munich, 1937), pp. 48–53.
[4] *Decline*, I, 46–47.

Originally the book was to have been entitled "Conservative and Liberal" and was to have been a political work primarily concerned with Germany. Twenty-one years later, in 1932, Spengler recalled how he had been "terrified" by the "folly" of his country's foreign policy, "which was calmly accepting the complete encirclement of Germany," by the "blindness" of everyone around him, by the "criminal and suicidal optimism" then prevailing.[5] As his ideas matured, however, their scope broadened. The emphasis began to shift from politics to the rhythms of culture. In 1912, the sight in a bookstore window of a history of the fall (*Untergang*) of the ancient world at length gave him the idea for the title of his own book.

Two years later, when the war broke out, the first draft of the *Decline* was completed. During the war years, Spengler revised and added to his manuscript. By 1917, it was ready for publication. But then began the "endless difficulties" of finding a publisher. After most of the prominent German houses had turned it down, it was finally accepted by Wilhelm Braumüller of Vienna. Of the original single-volume edition (the contents of a promised second volume were announced), only fifteen hundred copies were printed.

*   *   *

Both the conception and the title of Spengler's large work had come to him in a flash of intitution. And such was the basic character of his book. It was a sombre, murky vision of the doom of our civilization. At its center was the parallel—frequently hinted at before but never developed in so great detail—between our own time and the later centuries of the ancient world. This was the core of the book. The rest was embroidery.

With a characteristic lack of modesty, Spengler announced his program. Not only did he propose, by a new, comparative method of historical investigation, to reconstruct "long-vanished and unknown epochs, even whole Cultures of the past . . . in

[5] From the preface to Spengler's collected *Politische Schriften* (Munich, 1932), p. vi.

much the same way as modern palaeontology deduces far-
reaching and trustworthy conclusions as to skeletal structure and
species from a single unearthed skull-fragment." He also under-
took to foretell the future—to predict "the spiritual form, dura-
tion, rhythm, meaning and product of the *still unaccomplished*
stages of our western history." [6] Not since Hegel, a century earlier,
had any German writer set himself so ambitious a task.

Within this general program, Spengler established for his
book both a wider and a narrower goal. The broader purpose was
to work out his new method of historical interpretation by applying it to the different epochs and civilizations of the past. The
narrower goal was to determine the "state of West Europe and
America as at the epoch of 1800–2000," to analyze the "Decline
of that West-European Culture which is now spread over the
entire globe." [7] Quite naturally, it was this second aspect that
originally caught the eye of the public and has given Spengler's
book its enduring popularity.

Taken as a whole, the work would represent a new philosophy—"*the* philosophy of the future, so far as the metaphysically-
exhausted soil of the West can bear such." Toward this new view
of life, Spengler felt, the whole of nineteenth-century thought
had been striving. No other period, no other race of men could
even have conceived such a task, let alone achieve it: "We men
of the Western Culture are, with our historical sense, an excep-
tion and not a rule." [8] Centuries had to pass, however, before
Western man became ripe for this final revelation. Now at length
he was ready to receive the knowledge of his "*conscious* relation
. . . to history." [9]

With this apocalyptic note, Spengler announced that he had
reached the topmost range of his pronouncements. For the present, we need follow him no further into the breathless atmosphere
of metaphysics. Enough has been said to indicate the range and
variety of what Spengler was undertaking. *The Decline of the*

[6] *Decline*, I, 112–113.   [7] *Ibid.*, I, 26, 50.
[8] *Ibid.*, I, 5, 15.
[9] From the essay "Pessimismus?"; in *Reden und Aufsätze*, p. 71.

West was to be much more—or less—than a mere work of history. It was to be both a diagnosis and a prophecy. And, in addition, its author was to display himself as a participant in, and an example of, the rush of history that he was attempting to chart. As one French critic complained:

> He gives us a feeling of dizziness because he resembles an astronomer who, not content to know that the earth turns, also tries, in the very course of his celestial study, to *experience* in his own person the various movements of our planet.[10]

In studying Spengler, then, we must constantly be on guard against his bewildering shifts of character: now he is the sober historian; now the lofty seer of the future; now the cool, detached observer; and eventually the impassioned participant, forgetting in his excitement his former pretensions to objectivity. We must identify and learn to recognize all these contrasting roles. But it would be an error to analyze them in isolation from each other. In considering Spengler's work, we should constantly bear in mind the different levels at which he is writing. We must look at him simultaneously as historian, as diagnostician, as prophet, and as a symptom of our time. Only thus can we obtain a balanced view of his achievements and limitations.

*   *   *

In essence, Spengler's new way of regarding history consisted in rejecting the traditional succession of ancient, medieval, and modern times and substituting for it a study of comparative cultures or civilizations. Of these cultures, the two about which he knew most were the classical civilization of the Greeks and Romans, and our own Western society. What was traditionally accepted as ancient history Spengler redefined as the history of classical culture, plus a brief sketch of two preceding cultures, the Egyptian and the Babylonian, and the garbled account of a successor culture, unrecognized until he himself "discovered" it,

[10] André Fauconnet, *Un Philosophe allemand contemporain: Oswald Spengler* (Paris, 1925), p. 8.

which he called Arabian or "Magian." Similarly, the conventional medieval and modern periods, properly regarded, together formed the history of the West, with side-glances at such non-European societies as China, India, and Aztec Mexico. The traditional view, Spengler argued, represented a ridiculous distortion, a product of the pride and myopia of European man. The new method would put things in their correct focus. The Western European or American would be taught that the society in which he lived was no different in character from the societies that had preceded it, and that it, like its predecessors, was destined to pass away when its appointed time had been completed.

Spengler called his method "morphological." That is, it represented an application to history of the biologist's concept of living forms. Each culture, in this view, was an organism, which like any other living thing went through a regular and predictable course of birth, growth, maturity, and decay. Or, in more imaginative language, it experienced its spring, summer, autumn, and winter. This biological metaphor provided the conceptual frame giving unity and coherence to the rest.

Within each culture, Spengler insisted, certain basic attitudes permeated all of life and thought. Properly defined and understood, these attitudes would give the key to the history of the whole culture. While they could most readily be identified in the realm of aesthetics—in the plastic arts and music and, above all, in architecture—they exercised an equally pervasive influence over the forms of economics, war, and politics, and even over so unlikely a field as mathematics. To the historian who knew what to look for, the most amazing correspondences among all such fields of activity would suddenly spring to view. Taken together, these basic attitudes formed what one of Spengler's critics has called a "master pattern"—a characteristic cast of the human spirit working itself out in the history of every culture of which any record remains.[11]

All of these "master patterns" were different, and every cul-

[11] A. L. Kroeber, *Configurations of Culture Growth* (Berkeley and Los Angeles, 1944), p. 826.

ture formed a distinct bloc of spiritual and physical reality, clearly delimited from its predecessors, contemporaries, and successors. Yet each one went through the same morphological stages. As Spengler himself confidently announced:

> I hope to show that without exception all great creations and forms in religion, art, politics, social life, economy and science appear, fulfil themselves and die down *contemporaneously* in all the Cultures; that the inner structure of one corresponds strictly with that of all the others; that there is not a single phenomenon of deep physiognomic importance in the record of one for which we could not find a counterpart in the record of every other; and that this counterpart is to be found under a characteristic form and in a perfectly definite chronological position.[12]

This was a promise which its author was never able to carry out to the satisfaction of his more discerning readers.

Underlying Spengler's pseudo-biological structure of history, were a series of personal presuppositions and attitudes that gave his work its characteristic intellectual tone and were responsible for much of its attraction. First and most central, perhaps, to his style of thought was the concept of history as *"a universal symbolism."* [13] At Spengler's hands, the record of man's existence ceased to be a casual succession of events or a mechanical chain of cause and effect and became the ordered, majestic unfolding of the implications contained in a limited number of awe-inspiring symbols. This thinking in symbols broke sharply with the more usual notion of thought as a logical progression from one idea to another. Instead of proceeding in conventional fashion according to the rules of deduction, Spengler advanced by sudden jumps, by flashes of illumination, leaving the interstices to fill themselves in as best they might. In place of logic and sweet reason, he relied on "feel" and "intuition." He poured out his scorn on what he regarded as the philistine notion of man as a rational animal.

[12] *Decline,* I, 112.
[13] *Ibid.,* I, 46.

Spengler's conscious, unashamed irrationality reflected a profound scepticism. His own period he regarded as necessarily sceptical: a new understanding of human psychology had made any other attitude obsolete and impossible. He was to write in 1919:

> The nineteenth century was the century of natural science; the twentieth belongs to psychology. We no longer believe in the power of reason over life. We feel that life governs reason. A knowledge of men is more important to us than abstract and general ideals; from optimists we have become sceptics: we are concerned not with what should happen but with what will happen; and it is more important to us to remain in control of facts than to become the slaves of ideals.[14]

"Abstract and general ideals," then, Spengler found to be no longer either interesting or important. Mankind had never in fact acted on them: the mainspring of human action was something closer to the level of instinct—something that Spengler called "life" and that manifested itself in "facts." Having digested this new knowledge, the historian must adopt a fresh attitude. He must become a relativist. He must realize that "his 'unshakable' truths and 'eternal' views are simply true for him and eternal for his world-view." [15] Other men in other cultures had thought differently, and their ideas were equally "true" for their time and their society. More particularly in the field of manners and morals it was impossible to establish what constituted "good" and "evil" for all time. Faced with this embarrassing variety of intellectual and moral standpoints, the historian could only adopt an attitude of serene detachment.

Quite naturally, in view of his cyclical theory of human development and his scepticism about man's ethical potentialities, Spengler dismissed as an illusion the idea of progress in history. Democracy he considered a pious sham. World peace he regarded as both unattainable and undesirable. The twentieth cen-

---

[14] From "Preussentum und Sozialismus"; in *Politische Schriften*, p. 84.
[15] *Decline*, I, 23.

tury, he predicted, far from being the century of peace, progress, and democracy that his contemporaries imagined, would prove to be an era of tyranny, imperialism, and virtually constant warfare.

The foregoing ideas, electrifying as they might be, were not quite so original as Spengler supposed. Isolated in his dismal Munich lodgings, without acquaintance in the international *milieu* of philosophical speculation and social theory, the author of *The Decline of the West* was largely unaware of what his more sophisticated contemporaries were thinking and writing. Much of it paralleled or preceded his own discoveries. No doubt his formulation of them was both arresting and original. Yet most of Spengler's new theory of history was already in the air at the moment of his flash of revelation in the shadow of the Moroccan Crisis.

CHAPTER TWO

1911: THE INTELLECTUAL TEMPER

IF WE try to picture in our minds what the year 1911 means to us, we may produce a variety of contrasting images. Depending on our interests, the information at our disposal, our station of life, and our general attitude toward the world, these images will vary in precision and emphasis. Among all the rest, four will probably predominate. We may arrange them in ascending order of discernment and realism.

First and most pleasantly, 1911 may be viewed as the close of a recognized period in society and fashion—the last of such periods that the European upper classes would be permitted to enjoy. In May, 1910, with the death of Edward VII, the era to which that genial monarch had given his name had officially terminated. It had lasted less than a decade—but it had been very nice. For a few transient years the old aristocratic grace of living had come to terms with the comforts and conveniences that modern money and technology could provide, and together they had created a style of life which, while it might not compare in elegance with the eighteenth century, did rather better than its immediate predecessor, ill-famed to this day for vulgarity and stuffiness. Decidedly, the Edwardian period had its own gentle and peculiar charm. Like the decade of the 1780's, it savored more lovingly the "sweetness of life" through a dim suspicion that such things were about to vanish forever. Even today, older people, most of whom never shared in its more exalted enjoyments, look back on it as "the happy time."

Happy in a different way was this decade for those who thought of life in terms of political progress. In this second image, the year marked the climax of an era of successful struggle. Both democrats and socialists saw reason to congratulate themselves. The long-deferred promises of human betterment implicit in the expansion of machine industry were about to be realized. In Britain, the battle for Lloyd George's "people's" budget had just been won: the Lords, stripped of their power, were about to bow to the will of the electorate. In France, the Radicals, who in 1905 had emerged from the struggle for the separation of Church and State as the dominant party in the country, still felt secure in their tenure of power. The Socialists might be challenging them with increasing popular backing—but the Socialists too were a party of the Left and hence of progress. In Italy, the levers of authority had just been returned to the competent if not impeccably clean hands of Giovanni Giolitti. As in the past, he could be counted on to provide a well-tempered combination of mild reform and respect for the constituted powers. Here also the Socialists exulted in the conviction that their hour of triumph was not far off. Germany and Russia, it was true, figured as distressing eye-sores on the democratic landscape. Yet even in these countries there was reason for optimism. In Germany, the Social Democrats—the sober, disciplined, democratically-minded masses whom Engels had educated and Bebel had trained—were on the verge of their electoral victory in 1912. And in Russia, the Third Duma was making satisfactory if unspectacular progress in the direction of economic reform. With such convincing reasons for self-satisfaction, it was only a rare political reformer who paid sufficient notice to the warning signals with which the first decade of the century had closed: a wave of strikes in France, a depression in Italy—above all, militarism everywhere.

This disagreeable phenomenon of militarism predominates in the third image of the year 1911—the image of an observer with his eye on foreign affairs. To him, the arrival of the German gunboat *Panther* in the Moroccan port of Agadir would mark the beginning of three years of practically uninterrupted crisis.

Within less than three months he would see the Moroccan dispute followed by a war between Italy and Turkey. On this conflict in turn would follow the two Balkan wars, themselves to be succeeded by the fatal shooting at Sarajevo in June of 1914. The whole series would unroll as though according to a predetermined plan—and apparently without possibility of deflecting its course.

Finally, for the few who had eyes to see and patience to understand, the years immediately preceding 1911 had witnessed the intellectual creation of a new world, disquieting in its illogical, shifting outlines, yet bright with the elusive attraction of half-grasped evocations. Freud in Vienna, Pareto in Lausanne, and Sorel and Bergson in Paris had already reached most of their final conclusions. Between 1902 and 1903 Pareto had published his *Socialist Systems,* a withering attack on the "sentimental" ideology of the Marxists, which was to cause Lenin many a sleepless night, and was to serve as a kind of preliminary draft for the presentation of Pareto's fully-developed theory of sociology during the war years. In 1907, Bergson's *Creative Evolution* had given philosophy a fresh sense of the driving force behind living organisms. A year later, Georges Sorel, in his *Reflections on Violence,* had endowed political action with a new and aggressively anti-rationalist vocabulary. In that same year, the first International Congress of Psychoanalysis had symbolized the fact that Freud and his colleagues had virtually completed the elaboration of their revolutionary technique for probing the secrets of the human unconscious. Such thinkers as these, with their scepticism about the power of reason to control man's actions and their doubts of his capacities for moral and political progress, lived in a world far removed from the optimism and self-confidence of the popular writers, the men of affairs, and the leaders of parliamentary majorities.

*   *   *

Similar doubts had vaguely haunted the whole second half of the ninteenth century. Democracy and progress might be the slogans of the hour, but for a handful of aristocratic sceptics, such easy generalities rang with a hollow irony. For another fifty years, they predicted, all might still go well—but then democracy would turn and destroy itself. From our own perspective of a century later we have found new reasons to interest ourselves in the speculations of two of these writers in particular—the French political theorist and statesman Alexis de Tocqueville and the Swiss historian Jacob Burckhardt.

As early as the 1830's, in dissecting—not without sympathy —the new democratic society in the United States, Tocqueville had put to himself the anguished question: "Where are we going?" [1] With age and experience, his answers became more and more sombre. His service as a deputy in the revolutionary assemblies of 1848 convinced him—if he needed further persuasion— that democracy in Europe would prove to be only a way station on the road to a bleak and tumultuous tyranny of the masses. For Burckhardt too the revolution of 1848 had been the decisive personal experience. A year later he had already resigned himself to what he saw approaching:

> I have no hope at all for the future. It is possible that a few half endurable decades may still be granted to us, a sort of Roman imperial time. I am of the opinion that democrats and proletarians must submit to an increasingly harsh despotism, . . . for this fine century is designed for anything rather than true democracy. [2]

In the dignified, old-fashioned university town of Basel, Burckhardt, as from a beleaguered citadel, played out his role as the champion of the European humanist tradition. "We may all go under," he wrote. "I will at least seek out the interest for which I shall go under, namely the culture of Old Europe." [3] Age and

[1] Alexis de Tocqueville, *De la Démocratie en Amérique,* quatorzième édition revue et augmentée (Paris, 1864) I, 7.
[2] Jacob Burckhardt, *Briefe: zur Erkenntnis seiner geistigen Gestalt,* Fritz Kaphahn, ed. (Leipzig, 1935), Zweiter Teil, p. 185; salient parts of several of these letters are translated in James Hastings Nichols' biographical preface to *Force and Freedom: Reflections on History* (New York, 1943), a translation of Burckhardt's *Weltgeschichtliche Betrachtungen.*
[3] Burckhardt, *Force and Freedom,* biographical preface, p. 7.

further reflection only deepened his forebodings. In the latter part of his life, shocked by a renewed eruption of armed violence in the War of 1870, he sketched in letters and in lectures the more precise outlines of his vision of the future:

> What is most serious, however, is not the present war, but the era of wars into which we have entered, and on this the new spirit must be founded. Oh, how much that has been dear to the cultured must be thrown overboard as spiritual "luxury!" And how strangely different from us the new generation will grow up.[4]

Under these circumstances, the state would by very necessity become militarized. The administration, the schools, all public life would be remodeled to conform to garrison standards. Even the working classes—hailed as lords of the future by demagogues and professional revolutionaries—would not escape the universal process of regimentation:

> . . . I have a premonition which sounds like utter folly, and yet which positively will not leave me: the military state must become one great factory. Those hordes of men in the great industrial centers may not be left indefinitely to their greed and want. What must logically come is a definite and supervised stint of misery, with promotions and in uniform, daily begun and ended to the sound of drums.[5]

The result would be a "general levelling down" to a standard of personal and cultural mediocrity. All would grovel in the same anonymity. In this atmosphere of genuine distress, liberal Protestantism would "scatter like dust," and the more dogmatic forms of Christianity—with their philosophic pessimism and their cult of martyrdom—would rediscover the fervor they had displayed under the Roman Empire. Perhaps they alone would offer serious resistance to the new tyrants.[6]

[4] Burckhardt, *Briefe*, Zweiter Teil, pp. 336–337.
[5] *Ibid.*, pp. 348–349.
[6] Burckhardt, *Force and Freedom*, p. 345; biographical preface, p. 47.

For a new race of tyrants would infallibly appear. "We might declare the rise of great individuals an impossibility if our prophetic souls did not warn us that . . . the 'right man' may appear overnight—and all the world will follow in his train. . . . Long voluntary subjection under individual *Führers* and usurpers is in prospect. People no longer believe in principles, but will, periodically, . . . in saviours." These saviours will be men who will recognize no limits to their arbitrary power and who will rule "absolutely brutally." In a phrase that has justly become celebrated, they will be "terrible simplifiers." [7]

*   *   *

Nietzsche is the link between Burckhardt and Spengler. While men like Tocqueville and Burckhardt felt compelled to predict what they violently disliked, Nietzsche found a measure of virtue in the recurrence of barbarism that formed his image of the future. In his lofty, mercilessly critical perspective, the restoration of a certain barbaric simplicity and honesty appeared the only means of overcoming the moral slackness of an age he unhesitatingly condemned as decadent.

Burckhardt and Nietzsche had originally been fellow-professors at the University of Basel and had felt for each other a sympathy approaching friendship. But they gradually drifted apart, as Nietzsche, who had marked respect for his older colleague's ideas, began to interpret them in a "hard" and "demonic" fashion that Burckhardt could not accept. The latter, loathing power and what it did to its possessors, refused to subscribe to Nietzsche's cult of the superman, which he—mistakenly as it proved—took to be a political doctrine. And as the prophet of the will to power sank into madness, Burckhardt could only recoil from the intellectual wreckage he left behind.

In the 1880's, from his Alpine solitude, Nietzsche had launched before an uncomprehending world a new theory of morals and the purpose of man's existence. His fragmentary

[7] Burckhardt, *Force and Freedom*, p. 345; biographical preface, p. 41; *Briefe*, Zweiter Teil, pp. 451, 485.

writings—cast in the form of glittering aphorisms—had presented in rough outline a view of psychology that a half century
later was to become very nearly axiomatic. At the center of
human motivation, Nietzsche placed the will to power. In less
provocative language, he might have called it a yearning for
self-fulfillment. As an inexplicable, quasi-instinctive drive, it foreshadowed what Freud was later to call the "libido," and Bergson
the "élan vital." Thus Nietzsche, although himself a militant
rationalist, proposed a theory of human motivation that eluded
logical definition. It implied that most theories of behavior commonly dignified by the name of ethics could be dismissed as
rationalizations after the fact, and that what men really wanted
was something far less altruistic than they were usually willing
to admit.

In this view, the system of morality generally preached in
the Western World could lay claim to no universal validity. Far
from consisting of truths eternally ordained, it was simply one of
a number of moral codes peculiar to different times and peoples.
Like these other systems, the ethics of the West could be judged
only experimentally. And from this standpoint, the Christian
code of behavior came off rather badly. It did little to encourage
the will to power or self-fulfillment in the world of the flesh. On
the contrary, it was a "slave" morality of asceticism and other-
worldliness. A better moral code would be one that furthered the
development of the loftiest specimens of human personality. Such
had been the dominant ethical attitude of the Greeks, which
Nietzsche called "Apollinian"—a joyous, sun-drenched morality
that encouraged realistic thinking and exulted in physical beauty
and bodily health. At the same time, a valid ethical system would
encourage self-mastery and personal discipline. This the Apollinian ideal had also accomplished, when it had tamed its spiritual
competitor—the "Dionysian" cult of intoxication and abandon-
ment.

Yet the blighted society of the late nineteenth century could
scarcely absorb the heady stimulation of such paradoxical ethical
teachings. In the cramped, suffocating, miserably bourgeois

world of his day, only a restricted minority, Nietzsche insisted, could understand and carry out his message. A new élite must create the fresh values that the herd was incapable even of conceiving. This élite—a master race in the sense of common ideals rather than a common blood inheritance—would practise the virtues of personal daring and intellectual honesty. Secure in the knowledge of their own superiority, they would breathe the pure air of mountain tops and tread proudly on the bleak summits of lofty thought and action.

To comfort his prospective disciples in their moments of weakness and self-doubt, Nietzsche had nothing very substantial to offer. Perhaps the nearest he came to a message of consolation was in his revival and restatement of the classical doctrine of "eternal recurrence." All things human, Nietzsche affirmed, would eventually return to their origins and would run again through their previous course of change. This cyclic theory of man's destiny implied a rejection of both the after-life of the Christians and the dogma of progress on earth with which Nietzsche's rationalist predecessors had replaced it. Eternal recurrence was a hard, uncompromising truth, to be intellectually endured only by firm and lofty minds. Yet Nietzsche tried to make of it a source of exultation. The new élite were to be taught to accept their fate and in accepting it to will it as though they had chosen it themselves. They would learn to find a stern satisfaction in participating in the renewal of a cosmic pattern. Human existence, in logical terms, might be meaningless, but in terms of symbolic values, each life took on significance by figuring in its proper spot in a vast myth-drama. The individual who stoically carried out his assigned role would have done his part in maintaining in all their ordered beauty the eternal archetypes—the symbols of life and creation—which would ever recur so long as mankind inhabited this earth.

The next turn of the cosmic wheel would bring a renewal of barbaric values. This prospect Nietzsche could contemplate with equanimity—partly because his doctrine of eternal recurrence taught the acceptance of all past and future events; partly because he defined barbarism in spiritual terms, as controlled passion and intellectual integrity; and partly because he failed to anticipate to what unprecedented extremes the decidedly unspiritual barbarism of the twentieth century would eventually attain. Basically, what Nietzsche advocated was a radical moral surgery, which he regarded as the sole hope for revitalizing an "aging civilization" that had sunk into nearly total sterility.

It was in this sense that he wrote of his new élite. A mere handful of highly-endowed spiritual leaders, these intrepid individualists would rejoice in the creative power of youth and self-confidence. They would inaugurate a "new warrior age." From the dead-level mediocrity of late nineteenth-century democracy, there would emerge a breed of "tyrants." The new century would be an era of "struggle for world-rule." Such were Nietzsche's ambiguous prophecies: he would have been horrified to discover the crude and specifically political meaning that his successors—Spengler among them—were to give to his lyric pronouncements.[8]

* * *

After a decade of hopeless madness, Nietzsche died, fittingly enough, in the year in which the old century ended. To the official intellectual leaders of the 1890's he appeared an isolated and eccentric figure. He had simply done his writing ten years too early. The first decade of the twentieth century—on its more rarefied levels—was to belong to his spiritual heirs.

What united the advanced thinkers of this decade was a common conviction of the impossibility of knowledge and ideas free from non-logical preconceptions. Much as they might differ in their articulate philosophies, Freud and Pareto, Bergson and Sorel, were in agreement in affirming that the ultimate basis of human action lay below—or above—the level of logical thinking. Yet they were far from rejecting "reason" altogether. In

[8] Friedrich Nietzsche, *Jenseits von Gut und Böse* (*Beyond Good and Evil*), ¶ 80, 81, 92, 101; Walter A. Kaufmann, *Nietzsche: Philosopher, Psychologist, Antichrist* (Princeton, 1950), pp. 87, 316–317, 339, 362.

explaining their "intuitive" theories, they used with consummate skill the traditional methods of rational argumentation. All of them devoutly believed in scientific norms and conscientiously tried to apply the scientific method. As judges of human motivation, however, they hoped to push their knowledge a stage beyond the point where most eighteenth- and nineteenth-century thinking had left off.

In attempting to situate Spengler among his contemporaries, we may distinguish two main intellectual currents. The first is most familiar to us in the work of Freud. This type of thinking, primarily analytical, sought to clear away what it considered the errors and prejudices of the commonly-accepted interpretations of human activity. Such a purpose was apparent in Freud's emphasis on the unconscious, in his critical attitude toward conventional moral taboos, and in his implicit pessimism about man's potentialities for self-improvement. The more creative, dynamic aspect of his thinking he left in the form of fragmentary suggestions—at least during the earlier part of his life. Before the year 1911, Freud's speculations on the significance of myth and symbol had remained unsystematized. They stood out simply as guide-posts in the exploration of the psyche. Their long career of exploitation by popularizers and heretic disciples was still in the future.

The political aspect of this primarily critical approach found its most vigorous exponent in Pareto. His frontal assault on the rationalist ideologies of democrats and socialists betrayed the bitterness of a theorist who felt the current of the times running against him. With scorn and irony, Pareto sought to demonstrate that the professed ideals of reformers were simply rationalizations for more primitive motives. Whether these ideals actually stood for immediate and tangible interests, or for certain quasi-instinctive reactions of class solidarity, largely depended on individual temperament and the needs of each historical era. In either case, the basic forms of political sentiment remained the same: only the rationalizations varied.

With Pareto as with Freud, the implications of the theory of human motivation were what most of us would call pessimistic. In Pareto's view, man's political nature was unalterable. Despite revolutions and the reforming activity of demagogues, the lot of the masses remained as it was before. No regime could properly be described as popular. In fact, the whole notion of "the people" was simply another creation of sentimental ideologists. The mass of mankind could not conceivably govern itself; it was incapable even of understanding its own interests. Whatever the slogans under which a particular regime operated, each one was a more or less disguised form of class rule.[9] Political history, then, could be redefined as the history of élites and the vicissitudes they encountered in trying to cling to power.

Hence Pareto also came out eventually with a theory of cycles. These cycles were formed by the ups and downs, by the alternations, of ruling élites. However much such élites might try, they never succeeded permanently in maintaining themselves in authority. The strong, proud men who had seized power in a society would do their best to adjust to circumstances by developing the qualities of guile and pliability and by admitting to their ranks qualified and ambitious individuals from the masses. But eventually the sentiments of solidarity, the "ideals" to which they had originally owed their strength, would become diluted, and they would lose their self-confidence as rulers. A new élite possessing the required virtues of ruthlessness and loyalty would overwhelm them. The cycle would return to its beginnings. Such a theory of political and social behavior was obviously conservative in its implications. It taught the masses to despair of change, and the ruling classes to show resolution in maintaining their authority. It gave to the conservatives of Europe—who had been thoroughly beaten in the ideological battles of the nineteenth century—the theoretical basis for a most surprising revival. After a century and a half of intellectualizing about politics, Pareto's harsh realism represented a return to the wisdom of a Thucydides or a Machiavelli.

The second major current of early twentieth-century think-

[9] Vilfredo Pareto, *Les Systèmes Socialistes,* I (Paris, 1902), pp. 83–86.

ing went beyond the criticism of existing standards to undertake the definition of new goals. While Freud and Pareto followed Nietzsche in destroying idols and philosophizing "with a hammer," Bergson and Sorel acted on his injunction of finding positive affirmations in human existence. Bergson was convinced that by no simple method of logical analysis could any of the more profound truths of life be discovered. Only a more sensitive, more intuitive process that grasped the whole configuration of things could approach an apprehension of reality. Having dissolved the tidy universe of logical categories into an ever-changing and continuous flux, Bergson sought out the motive force behind existence. Quite naturally, what he found was inexplicable. His definition of it as an "élan" left no one much the wiser. But it served as a philosophical rallying-cry for those who wished to feel that in exerting their wills and manifesting their creativity they were conforming to a deep-running cosmic impulse, irresistible in its compulsion.

Among those experiencing the stimulus of Bergson's ideas, Sorel was one who frankly recognized his debt. A highly conscious revolutionary and a heretic Marxist, Sorel spent his later years looking for a *ricorso*—a renewal of history that would restore the barbaric virtues of pride and devotion. These, like Nietzsche, he defined in spiritual terms, as the integrity of the manual worker and the heroism of the religious believer. Sorel too was an élitist—though he hoped to find his élite among the militants of trade-unionism rather than in the European upper classes. And Sorel—perhaps most characteristically—redefined political action in terms of loyalty to symbols and remote myths that could never be realized. Sorel may well stand at the end of our roster of Spengler's predecessors and contemporaries. In him, the new ways of thought emerge in their sharpest form. Élite, barbarism, myth—the words ring out like a political catechism for the new century.

These words and practically all the ideas we have been surveying were to appear in pure or distorted form in *The Decline of the West*. But before taking up the disputed question of the sources of Spengler's theories, we should pause to look at the state of historical thinking in the first decade of the twentieth century —to trace in schematic outline the origin and vicissitudes of certain historical concepts that were particularly influential at the time Spengler himself began to write.[10]

[10] In my *Consciousness and Society* (New York, 1958), I have surveyed in much greater detail than was possible in the foregoing paragraphs the intellectual temper of the twentieth century's opening decade, stressing more particularly the efforts of Freud and Max Weber to salvage and to restate the rationalist tradition inherited from the Enlightenment, as opposed to the emphasis on pessimism and non-logical motivation that seemed appropriate in a Spenglerian context.

CHAPTER THREE

1911: THE HISTORIANS AND THE WORLD OUTLOOK

IN one of his characteristic all-embracing generalizations, Spengler differentiated between the attitudes toward history of classical and Christian mankind:

> It is well . . . to recall . . . that each of the different great cultures has pictured *world-history* in its own special way. Classical man only saw himself and his fortunes as statically present with himself, and did not ask "whence" or "whither." Universal history was for him an impossible notion. . . . Magian man sees it as the great cosmic drama of creation and foundering, the struggle between Soul and Spirit, Good and Evil, God and Devil—a strictly-defined happening with, as its culmination, . . . the appearance of the Saviour. Faustian [Western] man sees in history a tense unfolding towards an *aim*; its . . . sequence is a *dynamic* image. He *cannot* picture history to himself in any other way.[1]

In this case, Spengler's word "Magian" can be roughly translated as "early Christian." Together with the attitude of the medieval and modern West, it constitutes the Christian standpoint. Most contemporary historians of history-writing would not go along with Spengler in differentiating so categorically between these two attitudes. But they would probably agree with him in distinguishing the Christian from the classical approach. The

[1] *Decline,* I, 363.

Christian attitude they would define in similar terms as dynamic and directed toward an aim, as opposed to the static aimlessness of the Greeks and Romans.

Thus, for example, Karl Löwith, the author of a recent work entitled *Meaning in History,* has written of the Greeks that they were never "concerned with man's distant future. All their myths, genealogies, and histories re-presented to them their past as an ever present foundation." The ancients, to the extent that they philosophized about history at all, thought of it as a series of cycles. The subject of history, whether individual man or city state, forever ran through the familiar course of small beginnings, prosperity, overweening pride, and ruin. Christian writers, in contrast, have thought of history as an eschatology—in the sense of knowledge directed toward the final goals of mankind. These two attitudes, Löwith finds, represent a kind of ultimate in historical understanding. "It seems as if the two great conceptions of antiquity and Christianity, cyclic motion and eschatological direction, have exhausted the basic approaches to the understanding of history. Even the most recent attempts at an interpretation of history are nothing else but variations of these two principles or a mixture of both of them." [2]

In his *Idea of History,* R. G. Collingwood, while agreeing with Löwith in distinguishing the classical and Christian attitudes, has defined somewhat more closely the concept of history as eschatology. This attitude, Collingwood asserts, is concerned not only with the final ends of man's existence. Christian history is also, by very necessity, universal and apocalyptic. It must be universal—since the idea of a single omnipotent God implies an interest in all the territories and ages over which that deity has ruled. In contrast to the parochial histories of the Greeks and Romans, "it will describe how the various races of men came into existence and peopled the various habitable parts of the earth. It will describe the rise and fall of civilizations and powers."

Similarly, the central importance that the Christian must

[2] Karl Löwith, *Meaning in History: The Theological Implications of the Philosophy of History* (Chicago, 1949), pp. 19, 221.

give to the birth and death of Christ himself necessarily colors his whole view of history. It makes it apocalyptic—that is, "divided into two periods, a period of darkness and a period of light." The first of these eras will have a "forward-looking character, consisting in blind preparation for an event not yet revealed; the second a backward-looking character depending on the fact that the revelation has now been made." We Westerners have retained the imprint of the apocalyptic attitude—although most of the time we scarcely notice it—in our system of dating events before and after the birth of Christ. Such innovators as the founders of the First French Republic and the Italian Fascists secularized the same idea by inaugurating new calendars with their years of accession to power. As Collingwood reminds us:

> The apocalyptic idea became a commonplace, although historians have placed their apocalyptic moment at all sorts of times: the Renaissance, the invention of printing, the scientific movement of the seventeenth century, the Enlightenment of the eighteenth, the French Revolution, the Liberal movement of the nineteenth century, or even, as with Marxist historians, in the future.[3]

Most succinctly, perhaps, the Christian, the Western idea can be called linear, as opposed to the cyclic theory of the ancients. Wherever Western history might be bound, it was going there in a straight line. And linear the writing of history has remained, in the hands of most of its practitioners, until this day.

* * *

One way of characterizing the course of European historical writing from St. Augustine to the eighteenth century would be to describe it as a progressive secularization of the concept of history as eschatology. By the time that Voltaire and Gibbon came to write their elegant attempts at a rationalistic interpretation of the past, the consciously Christian vocabulary had virtually disappeared. Yet the Christian structure remained. The outlook was

[3] R. G. Collingwood, *The Idea of History* (Oxford, 1946), pp. 49–50, 52.

still eschatological: the eighteenth-century historians sought out the purpose of man—and found it in his advance toward reason. It remained universal: Gibbon surveyed the sweep of past ages and decided to interest himself in the decline and fall of a vanished civilization. And it could be called apocalyptic—in the sense that the apocalypse had been moved up to the present: the age of intellectual light and harmonious reason.

We need scarcely insist on the narrowness of a concept of history that judged every past event by a series of ready-made rational standards. In this view, history became a kind of proving-ground for the trial runs of what the eighteenth century had at length discovered to be reasonable and enlightened. All that the historian needed to do was to apply to a given slice of the past a logical explanation that had proved satisfactory in elucidating another segment of history to which it bore a superficial resemblance. By the middle of the century, the intellectual atmosphere was in grave need of an airing. In historical writing as in imaginative literature, this was provided by the Romantic movement. More than any other creative field, perhaps, the writing of history was to profit by the Romantic influence. Here the Romanticists' reshaping of critical standards was to culminate in the attitude that the Germans—its most articulate exponents—call *Historismus*, or "historism." [4] Basically, what the Romantic historians were seeking, and the "historists" believed they had attained, was a new sense of the richness and variety of the past. Rejecting the notion of simple and uniform explanations, they looked for what was peculiar to each time or people. They interested themselves in local traditions, in folk songs, in customary law, and in the origins of language. Crudely perhaps, but with touching good faith, they tried to convey a sense of the color and atmosphere of history. They loved the past—more particularly the Middle Ages, which the Enlightenment had scorned as an era of superstition— and conscientiously attempted to understand how the men of vanished generations must have thought and felt. In a flash of

[4] On this whole subject, see Friedrich Meinecke, *Die Entstehung des Historismus,* II (Munich and Berlin, 1936). For those who find my summary of eighteenth-century historiography overstated and schematic, I suggest as a corrective: Ernst Cassirer, *The Philosophy of the Enlightenment* (Princeton, 1951), Chapter V.

new understanding, they grasped what it meant for an idea or an institution to *develop*. To explain their discovery, they hit on a metaphor rich with possibilities and dangers for the future—the concept of organic growth. From now on, man's works were to be treated as near neighbors of the vegetable kingdom.

Yet the concept of organic growth was far more profound and helpful than anything that had preceded it. While it had its pitfalls, it represented a closer approximation to what a good historian can sense about the nature of historical change than any alternative figure of speech. And in general, it may be said of Romanticism that it was the decisive movement in the creation of our contemporary attitude toward the past. Despite their verbal and conceptual excesses, the Romantic historians were on the track of most of the major innovations that we have learned to associate with our own time: the study of art forms as a key to the spirit of past ages, the theory of non-logical motivation, and the notion of relativism in judging the moral and political behavior of past eras. The Romantic concept of history remained linear. But it was far less dogmatically so than the attitude of either the Christian writers or the historians of the eighteenth century. Had all proceeded without interruption, Romantic history, shorn of a certain pretentious naiveté, might have arrived fairly early at an essentially contemporary attitude of scepticism and a feeling for comparative values.

At this point, the botanical analogy—the plant theory of historical change—began to reveal its drawbacks. In the 1860's and 1870's, the study of history came increasingly under the influence of natural science. More particularly, the vogue for Darwin's theory of natural selection—usually misunderstood— occasioned a thorough-going re-interpretation of the concept of organic growth. Newly enlightened by *The Origin of Species,* historians were no longer content to view the development of human institutions as an illogical, largely aimless unfolding. Since the scientists had discovered a hitherto unsuspected logic behind the origin and survival of species in nature, it was now up to the historians to concoct a similar theory for explaining the rise and fall of nations. Such was not difficult to find. Obviously, in the struggle for survival, those peoples had come out on top whose institutions had best fitted them to compete with their neighbors. And, in the third quarter of the nineteenth century, the nation that appeared to have prospered most, by and large, was Britain. To what had Britain owed her success? To her representative institutions and traditions of freedom. Thus, to Anglo-Saxon historians—and to continental thinkers who felt themselves to be abreast of their times—the logic of history became the logic of liberalism. The pragmatic test of survival had proved that liberal institutions were best. This was the direction in which history was moving. More advanced historians would add that it was going beyond liberalism to full democracy—or even to socialism.

The outcome of all this was a partial return to the eighteenth century. In particular, the evolutionary viewpoint implied a rehabilitation of the idea of progress—which the Enlightenment had formulated, but which had subsequently been soft-pedalled by the Romantics. The notion of history as straight-line direction had now returned in full force. No longer could historians nourish the suspicion that the past was as good as the present—or even, perhaps, superior to it. Mankind had been proved to be on the march upwards. Democracy had established itself as the new apocalypse.

When strung along in this fashion, the mid-nineteenth-century ideas of evolutionary history, as exemplified in organic growth, natural selection, and progress toward democracy, align themselves in apparent harmony. Actually, the intellectual make-up of the more scrupulous among the heirs of *Historismus* was far less simple than that. Few went the whole way from Darwin to democracy. Most of them—whether from judicious caution or from mental sloth—kept their historical consciences and their political convictions in separate drawers. As historians, they limited their scientific borrowings to the notion that history was itself scientific. In their conviction that the study of the past should be pursued according to the methods of natural science, they exemplified an attitude usually called positivist. As good positivists, they strove for scrupulous accuracy in the ascertainment of "facts" and for objectivity in their presentation. They tried to write down no statement for which a good "source" was not available and to refrain from expressing an opinion until they had carefully analyzed the arguments on both sides. By this application of the scientific method, they reasoned, historians would eventually arrive at an accurate picture of the past. In their painstaking, frequently tedious researches, they were sustained by the conviction that historical truth existed and that its discovery was possible.

Yet underlying the work of these dry, judicious historians lay deep-felt political convictions. Such convictions might appear in articulate form only in the polemical essays and speeches with which the nineteenth-century historian relieved the monotony of his professional labors, or in the occasional paragraphs in his learned writings in which he summed up a major trend, but they gave tone and pace to his whole literary output. They reduced to near nonsense his professions of objectivity. The causes for which a historian of the 1870's or 1880's might be led to mount his charger and ride off to the attack were as various as the nations and political movements of the era. Beside the "advanced" creeds of democracy and progress, they included the cult of industrialism and the presumed virtues of the curiously contrived Reich that Bismarck had founded. Almost uniformly, the historian would discover in the early centuries of the nation to which he owed allegiance a suitable collection of chivalrous and picturesque qualities, worthy of celebration in the present. Characteristically, the historian's political reflections were as hasty and banal as his professional judgments were well-considered and original.

As a result, the historian of the latter half of the century thought and wrote on two widely-separated planes. The positivist, the would-be scientific historian, strove to recreate the true image of the past. The loyal citizen, the enthusiast, let himself be carried along by the currents of the hour. Between these planes, the traditional level of great history, the level on which historians who are at the same time philosophers have always sought out the spiritual origins of vast social and intellectual movements and, in understanding them imaginatively, have of necessity passed judgment on them—this level lay neglected. Western history was forgetting that it was by nature universal. In his positivist incarnation, the historian refused to commit himself; he was content to remain in the safe regions of external description. As a polemicist, he had nothing important to say. Thus, toward the end of the nineteenth century, as during the second half of the eighteenth, the writing of history was becoming arid and narrow. The lessons of *Historismus* were being drowned in the flood-tide of pseudoscience. A revolt was again in order.

*   *   *

Beginning in the 1880's and continuing until the present day, a succession of philosophically-minded historians have undertaken to restore history to its great level of comprehensive views and bold, meaningful generalizations. Among themselves they have differed greatly in their professional methods and articulate philosophies. But basically, they have all been striving toward the same thing: the restoration to history of its essential qualities of universality and imagination, and a rethinking in more radical terms of the relativist approach inherited from Romanticism. This revolution has not yet been completed. In any proper sense, it can never be completed. Indeed, the feeling of participation in so comprehensive an effort of intellectual renewal is what continues to encourage the efforts of the more thoughtful of present-day historians to rise above the level of mere antiquarianism.

Even in the most prosperous years of Darwinian history, a few writers held out against the prevailing current. Burckhardt—whom we have met already in the guise of a political sceptic—was one of them. In precise terms, Burckhardt rejected the notion of progress. "Neither man's spirit nor his intellect," he wrote, "has demonstrably improved in the period known to history." Rather than frantically pursuing the mirage of progress, Burckhardt advised, the historian should attempt to arrive at a sympathetic understanding of the spirit of past eras. The way to such an understanding lay through a study of art forms—and of architecture in particular. "The character of whole nations, cultures and epochs speaks through the totality of their architecture, which is the outward shell of their being." [5] Burckhardt's advice was sound, and three generations of later historians have acted on it. Almost invariably, the discerning historian of today holds Burckhardt in reverence as the most sensible and best-tempered of his masters. Yet Burckhardt was too urbane, too balanced to serve as the initiator of an intellectual movement of revolt. He too, like the positivists, refused to commit himself to any comprehensive theory of history. Having rejected all the more facile ways of looking at the past, he left his own interpretation suspended on "the thin thread of mere continuity." [6] He refused to move beyond scepticism to the construction of a new assortment of working hypotheses.

Far bolder and more dogmatic was the attitude that we may call neo-idealism. Prepared by the critique of *Historismus* with which Wilhelm Dilthey and Heinrich Rickert had upset the German historical world, it found its most articulate exponent in the Italian Benedetto Croce. Historical idealism, in the words of one of its devoted practitioners, means "the conception of historical knowledge as the re-enactment of the past in the historian's mind." [7] The idealists were ready to go along with the positivists in insisting on the necessity for scrupulous care in the location and assessment of historical data. But they were unwilling to stop there. They did not share the positivists' unsophisticated faith that by a simple process of painstaking research the essential reality of the past could be recaptured. In a healthy reversion to common sense, the idealists recognized that the past was dead and gone. It could never be recaptured. All that could be restored to life was the spirit, the way of thinking, the *idea,* of a vanished age. And to re-create this idea demanded an immense, a total

[5] Burckhardt, *Force and Freedom,* biographical preface, p. 56; text, p. 163.
[6] Löwith, *op. cit.,* p. 26.
[7] Collingwood, *op. cit.,* p. 163.

effort of imagination on the part of the historian. Hence the theory of historical writing advanced by Croce and his disciples was idealist in a double sense. It established the spirit of past ages as the essential reality of history. And it defined the task of the historian—beyond the menial labor of fact-gathering—as the intellectual re-creation of this spirit in his own mind.

In this way, out of a thorough-going scepticism, the idealists developed a new canon of historical method. Perhaps the most important thing about their theory was that it set history free from its bondage to natural science. In the idealists' view, history was either a branch of art, as Croce asserted in 1893 in his first important theoretical essay, or it was practically synonymous with philosophy, as Croce was eventually to conclude. It was scientific only in the sense that it followed its own rigorous procedure in the selection and evaluation of data. We can scarcely exaggerate the benefits that this fresh approach has conferred on the past two generations of historians. Yet, like any exclusive theory of history, idealism brought its own nemesis. Even in its original form, the concept of history as a re-creation of ideas was somewhat abstract and rarefied. Subsequently, as Croce grew older and his disciples—particularly in Italy—came to apply his method in an ever more mechanical fashion, idealistic history began to take off into a realm of pure spirit bearing only a tenuous relation to the world of verifiable experience. It became in its turn dry and unimaginative. Neo-idealism may be the single most illuminating theory of history that has been developed to date. But it has not exhausted the possibilities inherent in a field of study that is bound by its very nature to undergo a constant process of renewal.

*   *   *

A second aspect of the revolt against positivism, more lax, perhaps, in its intellectual standards than neo-idealism, but of greater relevance for the study of Spengler, was the revival of cyclical theories. The cyclical historians broke less radically than the idealists with the prevailing positivist tradition. All of them, in fact, remained within that tradition to a greater or lesser extent.

But they went much farther than the idealists in the vigor of their generalizations and in their willingness to raise on shaky foundations of evidence or hypothesis the most alarmingly novel historical constructions.

For this reason, the cyclical historians were, and are to this day, regarded with deep suspicion by the rest of the profession. Most of them were non-professionals themselves, gentlemen scholars and men of the world—or even (most suspicious of all) sociologists. They were more interested in discovering grandiose explanations for large events than in verifying their detailed evidence, and they loved to ride a theory to the farthest limits of its applicability. Much of what they wrote paralleled or was influenced by the anti-rationalist tendencies discussed in the previous chapter. Like Nietzsche, Pareto, or Sorel, the cyclical historians had sensed the possibilities inherent in the classical doctrine of eternal recurrence and had embarked on a systematic effort at their exploitation.

In so doing, these writers obviously upset the major premise of Western or Christian historical writing—the notion of straight-line direction. To this extent, they represented a throw-back to the attitude of the ancients. But not entirely: *within* each cycle, or separate civilization, they admitted the possibility of a goal. They retained the idea of direction, the dynamic quality of Western history, while drastically limiting its scope. The compromise was perhaps illogical. Yet it had behind it the example of the historian whom the cyclical theorists regarded as their original precursor—the twelfth-century monk Joachim of Floris. Joachim had divided history into three stages, that of the Father, that of the Son, and that of the Spirit, corresponding respectively to the Old Testament, the New Testament, and the promised future time. The originality of his scheme lay in his conception of correspondences between the different stages. Every event or figure in the Old Testament Joachim viewed as corresponding, in a spiritual sense, to a parallel event or figure in the New Testament. Each stage of history, he taught, rose to its own climax, and each successive stage naturally represented a higher level of spiritual development. Yet within each stage, the course of its unfolding bore a detailed resemblance to the course of its predecessor.

The other precursor whom the cyclical historians might have regarded with reverence was Giambattista Vico. Yet none of them recognized the extent to which he had anticipated their theories, and most appear to have had only a vague acquaintance with his work. An obscure, misunderstood Neapolitan professor of the early eighteenth century, Vico was so alien to the dominant spirit of the Enlightenment, and he cast his writings in so cryptic and difficult a form, that a century was to pass before his ideas could find a sympathetic understanding. It was only after the Romanticists had done their work of intellectual preparation that Vico could take his proper place in the succession of Western historians. From this standpoint, he may be regarded as the first "historist." As the tutelary deity of Benedetto Croce, he is also the spiritual father of neo-idealism. In fact, for a century and a half now, nearly every movement of renovation in the writing of history has fastened on Vico as its sponsor. His contributions to cyclical theory, then, do not remotely exhaust his permanent significance for the study of history.

To future cyclical historians, Vico bequeathed, in addition to the notion of cycles as such, a series of precepts for a more judicious understanding of the past. He warned against certain types of "pride" that had led his predecessors into error. He found, for example, that the "magnificent opinions" historians cherished about the Greeks and Romans caused them to exaggerate the virtues and achievements of antiquity. Similarly, he reproached his predecessors with an unwillingness to believe that a nation or people could invent, on its own, ideas or institutions resembling those of earlier nations; in accordance with what Vico called the error of the "scholastic succession of nations," historians kept insisting that each people must have learned these things from a people farther advanced on the path of civilization. Such a theory Vico rejected as obvious nonsense. In thus reducing antiquity to human scale, and in affirming the spiritual autonomy

of individual cultures, Vico established two principles that have
been fundamental to twentieth-century historical writing. And to
these critical precepts he added a number of positive canons for
an imaginative reconstruction of the past—the study of myths
and artistic monuments, for example, and the use of comparisons
between familiar historical developments and those known only
in fragmentary fashion, in order to fill in by analogy the missing
stages and details. Together, these injunctions made for the sort
of detachment and sense of relative values that we of today prize
as the historian's essential qualities.

As for the cycles themselves, the core of Vico's teaching was
the theory of *ricorsi* or historical returns—to which we have
already seen Sorel turning for moral inspiration. Each period in
a nation's history, Vico found, had a general character resembling
that of a similar period in the life of another nation, and from
this similarity it was possible to chart a typical course for the history of all peoples. Starting with a warrior or "heroic" age, they
passed through a major phase of true civilization, arriving eventually at a second barbarism. This new "barbarism of reflection"
was actually worse than the primitive "barbarism of the senses,"
since it was mean-spirited and over-subtle, where the character
of the heroic age had been generous and imaginative.[8] With the
advent of an intellectualized barbarism, civilized society had
reached its limits, and the cycle ended. Then came the *ricorso*—
the beginning of a fresh cycle—with a new heroic age. Such were
the European Middle Ages, which, to Vico's eyes, reproduced the
essential features of an earlier heroic age, the Homeric era of
antiquity.

Each new cycle, however, was not simply a repetition of its
predecessor. In the meantime, fresh cultural elements had appeared, which gave a new spiritual content to the *ricorso*. Thus
the advent of Christianity profoundly differentiated the medieval
period from its Homeric prototype. This concept of change from

[8] *The New Science of Giambattista Vico,* translated from the third edition
(1744) by Thomas Goddard Bergin and Max Harold Fisch (Ithaca, N. Y.,
1948), p. 381.

cycle to cycle has led some critics to describe Vico's theory as
more spiral than circular. Here again, as with Joachim, the sense
of direction, the dynamism, of the Western attitude toward history entered in to modify and enlarge the strictly cyclical concept
of the ancients. For, beyond the notion of direction within the
cycles, this view of history gave to the whole succession of cycles
an ultimate goal—the Christian apocalypse. To sincere Christians
like Joachim and Vico, history could not possibly appear as a
mere treadmill: that would have been blasphemy. Yet Vico had
too critical a mind, too fine a sense of comparisons and relative
values, to be able to write a dogmatic history of salvation. Like
his spiritual successor Toynbee, he was constantly pulled in one
direction by his critical faculties and in another by his Christian
conviction that history must point toward a higher goal.

Thus the theory of *ricorsi* that he left behind him was "all
broken up with exceptions." His infatuation with the history of
Rome—here again, a fateful legacy to his successors—led him to
force the history of other nations to fit what he regarded as a
typical pattern. His *New Science* was far more suggestive than
exact. It was an *ideal* construction, to be confronted only subsequently with the intractable data of history. As Croce reminds us:

> Rather than narrating or describing, Vico classifies. But
> there are classifications and classifications: those that are
> made in the service of a superficial thought and those that
> serve a profound thought. And the historical part of *The
> New Science* represents a great substitution of profound for
> superficial classifications.[9]

Such a dictum may properly stand for the majority of his
successors, and in particular for Oswald Spengler, whose best
efforts were directed toward the replacement of the conventional
historical categories by new groupings calculated to stimulate
both controversy and thought.

[9] Benedetto Croce, *La Filosofia di Giambattista Vico,* quarta edizione rive-
duta (Bari, 1947), pp. 130, 156. For a less schematic view of Vico, see Frank
Manuel, *The Eighteenth Century Confronts the Gods* (Cambridge, Mass.,
1959), pp. 149–167.

In the two decades before Spengler began writing the *Decline,* the brothers Adams, Henry and Brooks, were engaged in a series of melancholy speculations on the future of Western civilization. Misunderstood in their own country, and practically without influence in Europe, the moody Boston aristocrats lived in a vacuum of frustration. Isolated though they may be, their writings form a curious and revealing chapter in the history of cyclical theories.

Both never grew out of the positivist attitude—despite Henry's protestations of total scepticism. Yet they differed from the run of positivist historians in preferring physical and mechanical to biological metaphors. In this sense—as Henry recognized —they had passed directly from the mechanistic eighteenth century to the sceptical twentieth without ever becoming properly assimilated to the profoundly biological century in between.

Henry's theories both preceded and followed those of his younger brother Brooks. The succession of their experiments in discovering the "laws" of history began with Henry's "The Tendency of History," which he submitted as a letter to the American Historical Association in 1894 in lieu of a presidential address. In this first effort, Henry Adams did little but insist on the necessity for discovering such laws. Two years later, confronted with a large manuscript of his brother's, of which he did not entirely approve, he launched the Roman analogy that in later years was to become a familiar feature of his thought. "As I read the elder Pliny," he wrote to Brooks, "I am struck by the astonishing parity between him and you. He came about a hundred years after the military age ended, and the police age began. You write just eighty years after the same epoch." And Henry concluded: "Allowing for our more rapid movement we ought still to have more than two hundred years of futile and stupid stagnation." [10]

Brooks' work, *The Law of Civilization and Decay,* put in uncompromising terms the thesis that Western civilization was on

[10] Quoted in Brooks Adams' introduction to Henry Adams' posthumous volume *The Degradation of the Democratic Dogma* (New York. 1919), pp. 98–99.

the way out. With the gradual accumulation of what he called "surplus energy" within a society, Brooks Adams predicted that internal pressure would build up to a point of unbearable tension.

> In this last stage . . . , the economic, and, perhaps, the scientific intellect is propagated, while the imagination fades, and the emotional, the martial, and the artistic types of manhood decay. . . . At length a point must be reached when pressure can go no further, and then, perhaps, one of two results may follow: A stationary period may supervene, which may last until ended by war, by exhaustion, or by both combined, . . . or . . . disintegration may set in, the civilized population may perish, and a reversion may take place to a primitive form of organism.

And so, for our own civilization the verdict appeared inescapable:

> No poetry can bloom in the arid modern soil, the drama has died, and the patrons of art are no longer even conscious of shame at profaning the most sacred of ideals. . . .
>
> Decade by decade, for some four hundred years, these phenomena have grown more sharply marked in Europe, and . . . art seems to presage approaching disintegration. The architecture, the sculpture, and the coinage of London at the close of the nineteenth century, when compared with those of the Paris of Saint Louis, recall the Rome of Caracalla as contrasted with the Athens of Pericles, save that we lack the stream of barbarian blood which made the Middle Age.[11]

Dissatisfied with what he regarded as a lack of precision in his brother's scientific methods, Henry resumed the task himself. After having sent up a few trial balloons in his *Education,* he had developed by the year 1909 a complete "Rule of Phase Applied to History." In this essay, he divided the modern era into three periods, culminating in an Ethereal Phase, of pure, abstract,

[11] Brooks Adams, *The Law of Civilization and Decay: An Essay on History* (New York, 1896), pp. x–xi, 383.

mathematical thought. Since—by a rather far-fetched analogy
with the appropriate laws of physics—the length of each phase
could be presumed to be the square root of that of its predecessor, the end of our civilization was obviously descending upon us
at a vertiginous pace:

> Supposing the Mechanical Phase to have lasted 300 years,
> from 1600 to 1900, the next or Electric Phase would
> have a life equal to $\sqrt{300}$, or about seventeen years and a
> half, when—that is, in 1917—it would pass into another or
> Ethereal Phase, which . . . would last only $\sqrt{17.5}$, or about
> four years, and bring Thought to the limit of its possibilities
> in the year 1921. It may well be! . . . Even if the life of the
> previous phase, 1600–1900, were extended another hundred
> years, the difference to the last term of the series would be
> negligible. In that case, the Ethereal Phase would last till
> about 2025.[12]

Farther than this point, the temerity of no cyclical historian
has ever reached. It is more charitable to Henry Adams to forget
his pseudo-mathematical predictions, and to remember the fragmentary observations in which he sketched with lively awareness
the outlines of the approaching age. One of these—from his
original essay of 1894—had announced the dilemmas that the
cyclical historian of the twentieth century would necessarily confront in finding a hearing for his new theories.

> If a science of history were established to-day . . . I greatly
> fear that it would take its tone from the pessimism of
> Paris, Berlin, London, and St. Petersburg, unless it brought
> into sight some new and hitherto unsuspected path for civi-
> lization to pursue.
>   If it pointed to a socialistic triumph it would place us
> in an attitude of hostility toward existing institutions. . . .
>   If, on the other hand, the new science required us to

[12] Henry Adams, "The Rule of Phase Applied to History," in *Degradation
of Democratic Dogma*, p. 308.

announce that the present evils of the world—its huge arma-
ments, its vast accumulations of capital, its advancing materialism, and declining arts—were to be continued, exag-
gerated, over another thousand years, no one would listen
to us with satisfaction. . . .

If, finally, the science should prove that society must at
a given time revert to the church and recover its old foundation of absolute faith . . . , it commits suicide.[13]

All of these things, in one sense or another, Spengler was to
do. And he was to meet the consequences that his American
predecessor had foreseen.

*   *   *

With Nikolai Danilevsky, the writer who most directly anticipated Spengler's major theories, we return to the biological
interpretation of historical cycles. Danilevsky was a positivist, but
he came by his positivism more honestly than most of his literary
contemporaries, since he had proved himself a natural scientist in
his own right by leading a series of exploratory expeditions to remote parts of the Russian Empire. The enforced leisure of the
long winters between these expeditions gave him time for systematic reading and reflection in political and cultural fields. The
product of his meditations was a work of historical re-evaluation
entitled *Russia and Europe* and originally published in serial
form in the year 1869.

Alone among the writings of the cyclical historians, *Russia
and Europe* was primarily a polemic. It was written to buttress
with historical arguments the Pan-Slavist contention that Russia
was not properly a part of Europe and should discover her own
destiny independent of Western influences. What, after all, was
Europe? Danilevsky asked his readers. Europe was "no more
and no less" than the "area of the Germano-Latin civilization
. . . or . . . the Germano-Latin civilization itself." [14] It was

[13] Henry Adams, "The Tendency of History," *Ibid.*, pp. 130–131.
[14] N. I. Danilevsky, *Russland und Europa*, Karl Nötzel, tr. (Stuttgart and
Berlin, 1920), p. 20.

a cultural rather than a geographic entity. Only through a process of fallacious geographical reasoning had historians come to lump the development of Russia with that of the European West.

In the fashion of a trained zoologist or botanist, Danilevsky proceeded to examine the traditional categories of historical investigation—and particularly the familiar succession of ancient, medieval, and modern times. These categories, Danilevsky found, violated the principles of logical division applying in all the natural sciences. They made sense only when one considered the history of Europe as equivalent to that of humanity. If one reduced Europe to its proper scale, then one saw that the true "types" of historical development—what Toynbee was later to call the "units" of historical study—were not arbitrarily-divided ages, but real and easily identifiable civilizations.

To each of them, as to every living thing, a "fixed sum of life" was allotted. Each passed through the stages of childhood, youth, maturity, and old age, until in due course it died. Their number was limited. Only the following ten fully qualified as historical "types:"

1. Egyptian, 2. Chinese, 3. Assyro-Babylonian-Phoenician-Chaldean or Ancient-Semitic, 4. Indian, 5. Iranian, 6. Hebrew, 7. Greek, 8. Roman, 9. Neo-Semitic or Arabian, 10. Germano-Latin or European.[15]

To these one might add the Mexican and Peruvian, which died through violence in their early stages.

The development of each "type" or civilization conformed to five basic laws. The first three Danilevsky outlined as follows:

First Law. Every tribe or family of peoples identified by a language or by a group of languages whose resemblance is perceived directly, without deep philological explorations, constitutes an original historico-cultural type if it is mentally or spiritually capable of historical development and has already outgrown its childhood.

[15] *Ibid.,* pp. 39, 57.

Second Law. It is necessary that a people enjoy political independence if its potential civilization is to be actually
born and developed.

Third Law. The basic principles of a civilization of one
historico-cultural type are not transmissible to the peoples of
another historico-cultural type. Each type creates its own
civilization under the greater or lesser influence of alien—
preceding or synchronous [contemporaneous]—civilizations.[16]

To a present-day reader, the first two of these laws are doubtless
self-explanatory. The third raises one of the basic questions confronting all historians of comparative civilizations—the extent
and character of the influence of one civilization on another.
Danilevsky's answer represented a sensible compromise between
the virtual denial of such influence (a position that Spengler was
later to adopt) and the notion of the "scholastic succession of
nations" on which Vico had heaped his scorn.

In Danilevsky's view, a nation or civilization could influence
another in one of three ways. The first two—colonization and
"grafting"—were comparatively superficial and gave unsatisfactory results. The second, in fact, might be positively harmful to
the younger nation, since (and here again the metaphor was
botanical) one carefully cultivated branch simply exploited for
its own benefit the tree on which it had been grafted. The third
and only fruitful method of cultural influence was that by which
the Romans had learned from the Greeks, and the Western Europeans from both of the classical nations—"an effect that we may
compare to the influence of soil fertilization on the organism of
plants or . . . of improved nourishment on an animal organism." Such a method produced excellent results so long as the
younger society took from the older one only such things as stood
"outside the sphere of national character, that is, the results and
methods of exact science" and the "technical usages and achieve-

[16] *Ibid.,* pp. 61–62; for these laws, since I have not had access to the Russian original, I am using the translation given by Pitirim A. Sorokin in his *Social
Philosophies of an Age of Crisis* (Boston, 1950), p. 60.

ments of the arts and of industry." But political institutions, religion, and the like could foster national creativity only if they remained the spontaneous outgrowth of indigenous sentiments and traditions.[17]

For his fourth law, Danilevsky cited Greece and Western Europe as brilliant examples:

> A civilization of a given historico-cultural type reaches its fullness, variety, and richness only when its "ethnographic material" is diverse and when these ethnographic elements are not swallowed by one body politic, but enjoy independence and make up a federation or political system of states.

The fifth law set the limits to the creativity of each civilization:

> The course of development of historico-cultural types is similar to the life-course of those perennials whose period of growth lasts indefinitely, but whose period of blossoming and fruitbearing is relatively short and exhausts them once and for all.

All nations, Danilevsky maintained, initially went through a long "ethnographic" period of preparation. This was succeeded by a period of state organization, stimulated by threats from without. And on this latter phase, there followed an era of true civilization lasting from four to six centuries. Such was the period in Roman history from the Punic Wars to the third century A.D., and in Western European history since the age of humanistic revival and scientific and geographical discoveries.

> This period ends, however, when the creative activity of the peoples of a certain "type" dries up: either they relax with what they have already achieved, maintaining the legacy of antiquity as the eternal ideal for the future and growing old in the apathy of self-satisfaction (as, for example, in China), or they advance into antinomies and contradictions

[17] Danilevsky, *op. cit.*, pp. 71–72.

that can no longer be resolved from their point of view and that prove that their ideal (like all things human) was incomplete, one-sided, and faulty, or that unfavorable outward circumstances had diverted its development from its true course; in this case disillusionment grips the peoples and they sink into the apathy of despair. So was it in the Roman world at the time of the spread of Christianity.[18]

Where, then, in this predetermined course of cultural development and decline, did Western Europe stand? Not yet in decay, Danilevsky answered, but past its zenith. Europe was in that afternoon, that autumn, that period of middle age when the time of true creativity is past and the fruits of an earlier season are gathered in. Such a period, in Danilevsky's view, necessarily brought the most impressive cultural harvest. Unquestionably, the products of the nineteenth century were more numerous and better-adapted to their purposes than the corresponding creations of the sixteenth and seventeenth. Yet, more critically regarded, the nineteenth century would prove to be primarily an era of exact and applied sciences, systematically exploiting the guiding conceptions in philosophy and the arts inherited from the creative activity of the three centuries preceding. And on this era of autumn harvest there would inevitably follow the true winter of cultural sterility.

With Europe nearing its decline, Danilevsky triumphantly concluded, Russia and the Slavic world were at length free to create their own civilization. The artificial dependence of the Slavs on the Germano-Latins would soon be ended. And the young peoples of Eastern Europe would do what no nation had before accomplished: they would prove themselves creative in all the major fields of cultural and social activity. Just as each nation in the past had given its special imprint to the arts and even to the sciences in which it had engaged, so some had excelled in one field, some in another, but none in all. Even the Greeks, who had created the highest ideal of earthly beauty, had failed

[18] *Ibid.,* p. 79.

in the realm of politics. Only the Slavs could at length realize the full potentialities of humanity.

* * *

Except as a Pan-Slavist polemic, Danilevsky's *Russia and Europe* exerted practically no influence either on Western European opinion or on the writing of history. Although its five "laws" and their corollaries had anticipated most of Spengler's major conclusions, these same ideas, when they appeared in *The Decline of the West,* burst on the world as a surprise. In fact, most of the Western European interest in Danilevsky came as a consequence of Spengler's work. Significantly enough, the German translation of *Russia and Europe*—there is no English version—appeared just two years after the original edition of the *Decline.* For Danilevsky came too early. Writing in the full tide of mid-nineteenth-century confidence, he could appear only as the somewhat exalted apologist for a "reactionary" cause. A half century later, a great many things had changed. Danilevsky's ideas, or fragments of them, had become widely diffused. The intellectual world was waiting for someone like Spengler who could present these ideas in dramatic and compelling form. As Spengler himself was to assert, his theories were called for in the second decade of the twentieth century and at no earlier time. Three years before the outbreak of the First World War was the proper moment for an imaginative investigator to pull together all the scattered shreds of evidence suggesting that European society was on the verge of a catastrophe—the prologue to a series of greater catastrophes. Seven years later, after the catastrophe had occurred, the world was prepared to listen.

Yet besides repeating in more powerful language what Danilevsky had already written, Spengler ranged wider and saw farther. *Russia and Europe* may be a better-tempered and more sensible book than the *Decline,* but it lacks the sweep and depth of Spengler's inspired vision. Moreover, Danilevsky could afford to be good-tempered. As an enthusiastic propagandist for the Slavs, he could scarcely be much affected by the verdict of inevitable decline that he had passed on the Western European world. In fact, he necessarily rejoiced over it, since it opened the door to the cultural liberation of the Slavs.[19] Nor was the notion of decline as he presented it too painful for even its victims to accept; they could view with some equanimity the prospect of slowly sinking into peaceful, self-satisfied sterility. But with Spengler, as with any proud and self-conscious European among his readers, the picture of a decaying society as a stern world of tyranny and conflict could not fail to arouse the sharper emotions of bleak resignation, defiant acceptance of a warrior role, on the anguish of near-despair.

[19] In his forthcoming book *Danilevsky: A Russian Totalitarian Philosopher* —the first full-scale study of the man—Robert E. MacMaster stresses his protagonist's role as a metaphysician and ideologist of totalitarian rule, as opposed to the usual emphasis on his Pan-Slavism and cyclical theories.

CHAPTER FOUR

THE "DECLINE":
SOURCES AND INFLUENCES

H OW much did Spengler know of the work of his predecessors and contemporaries whom we have been passing in
review? The question is impossible to answer with precision. Spengler was not given to discussing the sources of his theories in any detail, and his practice in citing authorities was distinctly haphazard. No one of the major writers we have mentioned received even a footnote reference in the *Decline*—except
for Joachim of Floris, whom Spengler revered as one of the supreme architects of the medieval world-view, and Nietzsche, to
whom, as we shall see at the end of the chapter, the author of the
Decline recognized a particular debt.

Of his predecessors in the role of political sceptic, Spengler
was definitely familiar with both Tocqueville and Burckhardt.
The former he mentioned in one of his later writings, along with
Disraeli and Bismarck, as an example of those rare statesmen of
the nineteenth century who, "possessed of the true political instinct," knew where their times were heading and resolutely tried
"to prevent, moderate, or divert" what they saw coming.[1] The
latter he attacked as a "belated romanticist" with a one-sidedly
aesthetic view of antiquity.[2] But to neither did he attribute any

[1] Oswald Spengler, *Jahre der Entscheidung: Deutschland und die weltgeschichtliche Entwicklung* (Munich, 1933); translated by Charles Francis Atkinson as *The Hour of Decision: Part One: Germany and World-Historical Evolution* (New York, 1934), p. 118.
[2] *Decline*, I, 28.

share in helping to form his picture of a future era of wars and tyrannies that so much resembled their own forebodings.

To Freud, Spengler never referred—unless the contrast between the ideas of "totem" and "taboo" that appears several times in the *Decline* can be taken as an oblique reference to Freud's famous essay of 1913. Of Pareto, there is no mention anywhere, and it appears extremely unlikely that Spengler knew of his work. Up to the time of the war, Pareto's *Socialist Systems* had not aroused much interest in Germany. The parallelism between Spengler's own basic ideas, and the theory of non-logical motivation and the critique of "ideals" and conventional morality embodied in the work of Freud and Pareto, can almost certainly be regarded as no more than the product of a common intellectual inheritance.

The same conclusion holds for Sorel and Bergson. Although Spengler included Sorel among those he called "Socialists of higher quality and conservative ways of thinking," the reference is again from one of his later works [3] and does not necessarily indicate any acquaintance with Sorel's ideas at the time the *Decline* was written. On Bergson we have for once a specific denial of any intellectual debt. In the autumn of 1918, a few months after the original publication of the *Decline,* August Albers, who was to become Spengler's most faithful admirer, paid his first personal visit to his idol. He found him literally surrounded by Bergson's works. Spengler explained to his visitor that at the time he wrote the *Decline,* he had read of Bergson only a comparatively unimportant anti-German tract. But since his critics had been accusing him of plagiarizing Bergson, he felt that it was incumbent on him to familiarize himself with the French philosopher's writings.[4] The story has the ring of authenticity. If Spengler followed Bergson and Sorel in insisting on the inadequacy of merely logical analysis, and in viewing reality as a dynamic flux that could be grasped only by "feel" and intuition, the simplest and most likely explanation is that Spengler and his French predecessors had arrived at similar ideas quite independently.

[3] *Hour of Decision,* p. 133.   [4] Albers, *op. cit.,* p. 133.

When we come to Spengler's precursors as philosophical or cyclical historians, the verdict is at least as negative. There is no word in the *Decline* of either Croce or his master Vico—although it seems incredible that Spengler did not know at least something of *The New Science,* which by his day had become a familiar part of the German educational program. Of the brothers Adams, Spengler was obviously and understandably ignorant. On Danilevsky, the evidence is conflicting. According to Pitirim A. Sorokin, a Russian Professor Spet visited Spengler in 1921 and found Danilevsky's book on his library shelves.[5] But this was probably the German translation, which had appeared in the previous year. Thus, while Spengler may have used Danilevsky in preparing his second volume and the revised version of his first volume, he had probably not read *Russia and Europe* when he wrote the earlier version of the *Decline.* We know that during his university days Spengler had associated with a group of Russian students and had learned something of the Russian language. But we are not sure how well he actually read it. Nowhere in the *Decline* are there any clear references to works in Russian, and the sole evidence for Spengler's knowledge of the Russian language is some brief discussion of the special significance of a few Russian words.[6] We may conclude that Spengler knew enough Russian to have some general ideas about the character of the language but not enough to read a Russian book consecutively.

On the other side of the question, Sorokin points out that Spengler was familiar with the works of such Slavophils as Sergei and Ivan Aksakov. But the only reference to the former in the *Decline* is an approving note explaining the hostility toward Europe that he shared with Dostoyevsky and Tolstoy—and, Spengler might have added, with Danilevsky. As for the other Aksakov, we find nothing more than a quotation in a similar vein from a letter he wrote to Dostoyevsky in 1863.[7] Since Dostoyevsky was Spengler's major source of knowledge for things

[5] Sorokin, *op. cit.,* p. 329n.
[6] For example: *Decline,* I, 309n.; II, 295–296n.
[7] *Ibid.,* I, 16n.; II, 193.

Russian, it is not too far-fetched to presume that the latter—at least when he wrote his original version—had heard of the other Slavophils or Pan-Slavists largely through his reading of Dostoyevsky in translation. Thus the most logical conclusion is that Spengler's original—and decisive—acquaintance with Danilevsky's theories did not extend beyond a vague and second-hand knowledge of their general outlines.

Albers, who knew a good deal about Spengler's writing habits, reports that his friend did not even know the titles of many of the books from which his critics accused him of stealing his ideas. He drew more on his knowledge of art than on the writings of his "so-called predecessors," and he was under no obligation to give them credit for theories that he had worked out himself.[8] This represents an extreme statement of a fairly defensible point of view. Obviously with Spengler, no more than with any other writer, can we discover a recognizable paternity for each individual idea; to attempt to do so would be to fall into the most pedestrian sort of positivist method. Even if an author himself were to try to explain the sources of his theories, he could not possibly disentangle what he had learned from others from what he considered original: the two would long before have fused themselves into the same tight and continuous pattern of thought. In Spengler's case, in addition to their common descent from Nietzsche, the author of the *Decline* and his contemporaries were writing in the same intellectual atmosphere of tottering standards, and values that were being questioned on all sides; they sensed the same break-up of society and intellectual life and the striving toward the surface of a primitivism that defied explanation in rational terms. They were all groping for a new style of thought, a new vocabulary, new definitions to express what they were sure was happening but could scarcely hope to make intelligible to readers trained in the traditional categories of logical exposition. Almost inevitably, their conclusions showed a certain family resemblance.

Since Spengler worked in greater intellectual isolation than

[8] Albers, *op. cit.,* p. 133.

Sorel, Pareto, and the rest, he wrote in a more personal style than they but with less critical discernment. As a consequence there is much that is curiously old-fashioned about *The Decline of the West*. Actually, Spengler knew more about the positivist historians of the previous generation than about the contemporary writers whose ideas most resembled his own. Many of his historical preconceptions were naively and unashamedly positivist. His "discovery" of morphological history was simply a pretentious blowing-up of the biological or botanical metaphor that had haunted the whole nineteenth century. Much as he might declaim against the "trivial optimism of the Darwinian age," his own conception of organic struggle and growth did not differ too widely from that of Darwin's popularizers.[9] Only in his more sceptical moments did Spengler doubt that there was such a thing as a retrievable historical past—or at least that it was possible to know the past of the individual culture in which the historian himself was a participant. The question of the extent of Spengler's positivism has been much debated and will reappear at intervals throughout this study. For the present, we must reserve judgment until we have examined in greater detail the contents of the *Decline* itself.

*   *   *

When we turn to the more prosaic and verifiable sources of Spengler's knowledge, the first thing that may strike us is his intimate acquaintance with the literature of antiquity. Like nearly all the social systematizers of modern Europe, Spengler was a trained classical scholar. Like Machiavelli, like Montesquieu, like Hegel, he drew his guiding examples from this store of narrative and drama that today is becoming a closed book even to the educated. His doctor's thesis on Heraclitus was a slight but respectable job of classical scholarship—with a touch of originality besides. In it we find a number of the leading ideas that were to reappear in more developed form in the *Decline*: the reliance on

[9] "Pessimismus?"; *Reden und Aufsätze*, pp. 73–74.

intuitive "feel" for an understanding of the past; the interpretation of Heraclitus' famous dictum "everything flows" as the key formula for a radical philosophic relativism; the exploitation of Nietzsche's theories about eternal recurrence and the "Apollinian" spirit of the Greeks; the treatment of a whole culture as an organic individuality and the affirmation of a necessary incompatibility between the basic concepts of one culture and those of another; the insistence on the contrast between aristocracy and the masses, on fate and determinism, and on the imperative need for a "hard" philosophy of life.[10] This was the picture of antiquity that Spengler had already worked out as early as 1903. It expressed his vigorous opposition to what he regarded as the feeble sentimentality of the aesthetic school of classical learning.

The faculty of the University of Halle evidently considered that *Heraclitus,* although primarily a philosophical essay, was a sufficient indication of Spengler's proficiency in the natural sciences, which had been his major field of study. Like Danilevsky, Spengler differed from most positivist historians in knowing what he was talking about when he drew analogies from the natural sciences. But while Danilevsky and his contemporaries were more or less well versed in biology, botany, or zoology, Spengler concentrated on mathematics. This mathematical training was to find a rather surprising outlet in the chapter entitled "The Meaning of Numbers," perhaps the most provocative section of the whole *Decline.*

After his knowledge of classical literature and mathematics, the decisive element in Spengler's intellectual formation was his very real feeling for art and music. The depth and sincerity of his appreciation are beyond question; they find eloquent expression in countless passages of the *Decline.* We scarcely need speculate on the possible sources of this enthusiasm. They were everywhere: in the Germany of the first third of the present century, the appreciation of cultural values achieved an almost unprecedented combination of wide diffusion and the maintenance of rigorous standards. The influence of music flowed in from all

[10] "Heraklitus" is included in *Reden und Aufsätze,* pp. 1–47.

sides. Munich, where Spengler had chosen to live, was a recognized artistic and literary center. For Spengler's appreciation of painting, sculpture, and architecture, his trips to Italy, as in the case of so many young Germans, doubtless gave the decisive impetus. Yet his feeling for the architecture of his own country —more particularly for the Rhine cathedrals and the Baroque of Bavaria and Dresden—became at least as strong. Of French and English art and architecture, his knowledge and appreciation were more superficial. During his period of teaching, he had travelled in France, but he never went to England. In fact, at the time he wrote the *Decline,* the only foreign countries he had visited were Italy, France, Austria, and Switzerland. When we consider the comparative narrowness of Spengler's first-hand knowledge, we are all the more struck by his acute sense for artistic style as the expression of inner cultural values, and by his feeling for the essential quality of artistic monuments that he could have known only from books and photographs.

His acquaintance with European literature was broad and substantial. Into the *Decline,* Spengler poured a wealth of reference to medieval epic poetry, to the French and Spanish drama of the seventeenth century, and—again a mark of the conventionally-educated German—to Shakespeare and Goethe as the two supreme masters of "Faustian" expression. He knew all the standard philosophers from Aquinas to Schopenhauer, he knew the British economists and Karl Marx, he knew the major poets from Dante to Baudelaire. For the recent period, his reading was less catholic. Here he relied most heavily on Ibsen, Dostoyevsky, and Shaw, professing for the latter two a nearly limitless admiration. Most of these authors he had doubtless read in the original language. Besides his native tongue, he had mastered the two classical languages and French. Yet, so far as France was concerned, Spengler's travel and linguistic knowledge do not appear to have given him a real feeling for the Gallic tradition: France and the United States were perhaps the only important nations, present or past, for which he never attained any sort of sympathetic understanding. In addition to the languages with which he was thoroughly familiar, Spengler read English and Italian, and had a more superficial acquaintance with Spanish and Russian.

It would be virtually impossible, of course, for any one human to have an adequate linguistic preparation for the sort of study that Spengler had undertaken. His own equipment, though incomplete, was perfectly respectable. What his critics were later to hold against him was not so much the inadequacy of his professional tools as the fragmentary and spotty character of his research. In the original first volume of the *Decline,* Spengler had given few specific source references. Perhaps owing to the goading of his critics, he provided the second volume with a far more elaborate display of scholarly paraphernalia. Yet even this did not satisfy the specialists. It indicated that Spengler had read widely in the writings of the German historians slightly senior to him in age—to the classicist Eduard Meyer, the only one of the professionals who was later to give the *Decline* a qualified endorsement, he referred with particular respect—and that he had conscientiously digested the available manuals for the history of art, linguistics, literature, and religion. But his references likewise demonstrated that when he had ventured outside the fields previously explored by the standard German historians, he had found only the shakiest support. He frankly recognized, for instance, that virtually his total knowledge of the culture of ancient Mexico came from two recent American works on the subject.[11] On the civilization of China he was only slightly better informed. And in interpreting the course of Arabian and Persian society from the decay of Rome to the advent of Mohammed he had stretched the fragmentary data at his disposal to the furthest bounds of credibility. Much as Spengler might decry the exclusively classical and European emphasis of his predecessors, his own intellectual preparation remained largely within the conventional groove. He could not escape the general preoccupation with Greece, Rome, and Western Europe—the only societies which his scientific and cultural training had adequately equipped him to understand.

[11] *Decline,* II, 44*n*.

In the preface to his revised edition of 1923, Spengler named Goethe and Nietzsche as the two writers to whom he owed "practically everything." From Goethe he had learned "method," from Nietzsche "the questioning faculty." [12] There is nothing particularly novel in this choice of masters. Thousands of cultivated young Germans of Spengler's generation might have made a similar declaration. We find originality only in the distinctive sources of inspiration that Spengler selected from the writings of his two spiritual guides.

In contrast to the vast majority of his predecessors and contemporaries, Spengler took seriously Goethe's pretentions as a natural scientist. Rather than dismissing them as the amateurish vagaries of a self-conscious old sage, Spengler found in Goethe's theories the model for his own "morphological" method. He admired Goethe's practice of contemplating natural phenomena in their total configuration. Like him, Spengler argued, the historian should seek out the *Urphänomen,* or prime phenomenon, that would reveal the spiritual depths of a whole civilization. And he should take to heart Goethe's warnings against the dissecting type of analysis that kills rather than illuminates its object. What analysis could never discover, a deep, intense contemplation might reveal. As a summary of his own "entire philosophy," Spengler quoted Goethe's declaration to Eckermann:

> The Godhead is effective in the living and not in the dead, in the becoming and the changing, not in the become and the set-fast; and therefore, similarly, the reason (*Vernunft*) is concerned only to strive towards the divine through the becoming and the living, and the understanding (*Verstand*) only to make use of the become and the set-fast.[13]

Thus, in Spengler's view, what the historian could learn from Goethe the natural scientist would eventually merge with the lessons of Goethe the philosopher. And behind the injunc-

---

[12] *Ibid.,* I, xiv.
[13] *Ibid.,* I, 49n.; Hildegard Kornhardt, "Goethe und Spengler," *Archiv für Rechts- und Sozialphilosophie,* XXXVIII/4, June 1950, p. 594.

tion to imaginative contemplation, there lay a further precept
of philosophical apprehension. "Alles Vergängliche ist nur ein
Gleichnis"—"everything transitory is only a metaphor:" the final
chorus of Goethe's *Faust* rang out again and again in the *Decline*
as its most pervading *leitmotif*. All things human, all historical
events, its author implied, were only passing reflections of great
hidden truths. From Goethe, Spengler had learned to view history as a shadow-play of appearances in which the tangible world
of events and ideas could do no more than suggest in fragmentary
and partial form the eternal spiritual architecture of the universe.

Interpreted in this fashion, Goethe's celebrated verse became the poet's sibylline method of enunciating the doctrine of
historical relativism. And such an interpretation is substantially
correct. As he paralleled the first Romantic historians in time,
so Goethe in spirit shared and helped to form their appreciation
of comparative values in history. Like them, he viewed the
"truths" of man's experience as shifting and changing with each
generation; like them, he shrank from denying that below these
surface opinions there lay more substantial truths, admittedly
vague in outline, but with a justified claim to absolute validity.
Through Goethe, the lessons of *Historismus* had reached Spengler
in their least methodical and most exalted form.[14]

To that point Goethe could help Spengler along the path of
understanding but no farther. The latter might give his master
credit for anticipating the idea of "spiritual epochs" in the life of
a culture, and he might see in the contrast between the first and
the second parts of *Faust* an epitome of the things that separated
the earlier era of creative thought from the "purely practical, far-
seeing, outward-directed activity" of the nineteenth and twentieth
centuries.[15] But in this very contrast, Spengler revealed the source
of Goethe's limitations. As the last universal literary creator of
the West, who in his sure sense of form represented the climax of

[14] Eberhard Gauhe, in his *Spengler und die Romantik* (Berlin, 1937), has
traced the parallelism between Spengler's leading ideas and those of the German
Romanticists.

[15] *Decline*, I, 354; II, 37n.

his own culture, Goethe had closed an era. He could depict the new century through the symbol of its ideal man, but he could never really live in it. And so, another hundred years later, while he could still charm and even teach the men of the twentieth century, he no longer had the power to change the way they actually felt and lived.

This Nietzsche could do. In a lecture appraising Nietzsche's relation to his century, Spengler defined the contrasting roles to which the accident of their birth-dates had destined his two spiritual mentors.[16] Goethe, rooted in the eighteenth century although living far into the nineteenth, could still share and affirm the values of his own time. Nietzsche, born a century later, was condemned to stand out against his era. Indeed, he was the only writer of the nineteenth century who consistently resisted the pressure of intellectual fashion. And in so doing, Spengler found, he became the teacher not only of those who, like the author of the *Decline,* felt themselves to be the prophets of "thoughts out of season," but of all of us, "whether or not we want it, whether or not we know him." The "melody" of Nietzsche's vision continued to influence us all.

And melody was perhaps the most rewarding of the historical insights that Spengler had inherited from Nietzsche. Alone of the great German thinkers, Spengler noted, Nietzsche had been a "born musician." Half-blind, he had "lived, felt, thought with his ears. . . . And so what he felt in past ages was their melody, their tempo. He discovered the *key* of strange cultures." Thus it would be a mistake, Spengler argued, to take too literally the suggestions for historical interpretation—like the notion of eternal recurrence—that Nietzsche had formulated. They should be treated as music. In his role of cultural diagnostician, Nietzsche should be esteemed for the imaginative use to which he had put his sources, for his psychological method, for his discovery of the "mighty symbols" that proclaimed the future. He should not be subjected to a petty grubbing for mistakes. For it was "beyond

[16] This lecture, dating from 1924 and entitled "Nietzsche und sein Jahrhundert," is included in *Reden und Aufsätze,* pp. 110–124.

and often in contradiction to the sources" that Nietzsche had
made some of his most profound discoveries—among them, the
formula that for the first time had penetrated the secrets of the
Greek soul: the "Apollinian" ideal, and its opposite in the dark
strivings of the "Dionysian underworld" of Hellenic culture.

For such lessons as these—eternal recurrence, the Apollinian spirit, and along with them, the integral view of cultures
and the emphasis on "individuals and classes born to rule"—
Spengler gladly recognized the unique debt he owed to Nietzsche.
And there were other things that he might have added to the list:
his notion of philosophical descent from Heraclitus, his hostility
to the Darwinian theory of progress, and his highly personal, non-
biological concept of race and "style." This massive philosophical
inheritance clearly indicates how carefully Spengler had read his
Nietzsche. Indeed, Nietzsche's lessons permeated the whole in-
intellectual structure of the *Decline*. In defining history as *"a universal symbolism,"* Spengler proved that he had understood the
essence of Nietzsche's "supra-historical" view—the establishment
of certain supreme specimens of humanity as a historical ultimate,
standing out above time and change.

In other respects, however, Spengler sharply diverged from
Nietzsche. As a political writer, the author of the *Decline,* like
nearly all other confessed Nietzscheans, hardened and distorted the lessons of the master. In his attitude toward the state,
Spengler reversed his predecessor's position. Where Nietzsche had
expressed open hostility to the state—and more particularly to
the new German Reich—Spengler placed the state in the center
of his historical scheme and never wavered in his loyalty to the
German imperial tradition. Here Spengler proved himself far
more conservative than Nietzsche. Indeed, he showed that he was
conforming with surprising docility to the tradition of nineteenth-
century German historical writing, which since Hegel's day had
organized history around the idea of the state. And like Hegel,
Spengler subordinated the role of the individual to the working
of vast historical processes—in diametrical opposition to
Nietzsche, for whom the individual represented the supreme

moral value. In thus bringing Nietzsche's prophecies down to the level of political "facts," Spengler took the decisive step before which his predecessor had recoiled in alarm: he made of them the joyous, welcoming proclamation of an age of barbarism.[17]

A suggestion, at least, of this divergence appeared in the passages of the *Decline* in which Spengler criticized his philosophical master. Even Nietzsche, Spengler asserted, was unable to grasp the full implications of the new attitude he had proclaimed. Like Goethe, he had stopped short of final comprehension. Nietzsche's historical horizon, Spengler found, had remained enclosed within the limits of the traditional categories:

> His conceptions of decadence, militarism, and transvaluation of all values, the will to power, lie deep in the essence of Western civilization and are for the analysis of that civilization of decisive importance. But what, do we find, was the foundation on which he built up his creation? Romans and Greeks, Renaissance and European present, with a fleeting and uncomprehending side-glance at Indian philosophy— in short "ancient, medieval and modern" history. Strictly speaking, he never once moved outside the scheme. . . .

Hence Nietzsche, although "the first to have an inkling" that there existed as many moral systems as there were cultures, "never came anywhere near to a really objective morphology" of ethics. He continued the traditional practice of making personal judgments on the morality of past ages and of his own time. By insisting on the relative character of all moral values, Nietzsche

[17] Kaufmann, *op. cit.*, pp. 101, 125, 260, 269, 288, 364n., 368. Although Spengler recognizes no specific debt to Hegel, his work shows the characteristic marks of what a contemporary critic has called Hegelian "historicism," in the following three related ideas: first, that "the way of obtaining knowledge of social institutions such as the state is to study . . . the history of its 'Spirit;' " second, that "the Spirit of the nation determines its hidden historical destiny;" and third, that "every nation that wishes 'to emerge into existence' must assert its individuality or soul . . . by fighting the other nations," the "object of the fight" being "world domination." In fact, Spengler figures as the most dreadful example of this sort of "historicism." See Karl R. Popper, *The Open Society and Its Enemies*, revised edition (Princeton, 1950), pp. 56, 233.

took "the first and essential step towards the new standpoint." Yet he "failed to observe his own condition;" he failed to "place himself 'beyond good and evil'. He tried to be at once sceptic *and* prophet, moral critic *and* moral gospeller." Quite understandably, he could not do both. And so, Spengler concluded, while Nietzsche knew what to deny, he could not see far enough to know what to affirm. "It is of the deepest significance that Nietzsche, so completely clear and sure in dealing with what should be destroyed, what transvalued, loses himself in nebulous generalities as soon as he comes to discuss the Whither, the Aim."

Since Nietzsche had collapsed into madness, a quarter of a century had passed. It had at length become possible to encompass in one view the whole historical horizon. This, Spengler announced, had been his own achievement—to widen Nietzsche's prophetic "outlook" into a total survey of the destiny of Western man.[18]

[18] *Decline*, I, xiv, 24, 315, 346, 363.

CHAPTER FIVE

THE "DECLINE":
THE MORPHOLOGY OF CULTURE

SIX months after the original publication of the *Decline,* the first printing had sold out. A second, then a third printing followed. Beginning with the third printing, the book was taken over by C. H. Beck of Munich, who was to remain Spengler's permanent publisher. Although the author had worked out the contents of his second volume as early as 1917, the book itself did not appear until April 1922. Meantime, the first volume had gone out of print. Spengler, who had been working on its revision since the end of 1920, refused to have the original version reissued. In early 1923, the revised first volume appeared, "greatly altered in its outward form, but unchanged in its basic ideas." Such is the explanation for the curious fact that in the definitive German edition the first volume is dated one year later than the second.

The actual composition of the second volume had been somewhat more rapid than that of the first. Spengler had dictated it from notes, then corrected it, and sent it directly to the printers. He had changed very little in galley-proof, and nothing in page-proof.[1] Perhaps for this reason, the second volume seems looser and more discursive than the first. Its predecessor had enunciated nearly all Spengler's basic ideas and given them their more original elaborations. The second took up again the same thoughts more or less from the beginning with a series of general reflec-

[1] Albers, *op. cit.,* pp. 132, 134.

tions on landscape, cities, peoples, and classes. On such controversial topics as the "Magian" culture and the nature of the state, it added special sections giving detailed evidence in support of theories previously thrown out as undocumented assertions. The long chapter on the state was actually a reworking of the earliest part of the whole work—the political treatise that Spengler had originally intended to write.[2] This chapter, which formed a self-contained unit, Beck was later to publish in separate book form. Other parts, like the section on Roman law, were cast in a style of contemporary polemic far removed from the aloofness of the first volume and anticipating the sharply controversial manner of Spengler's political writings.

In its final version, then, *The Decline of the West* is annoyingly long and repetitious. It never seems to have occurred to Spengler that his theories might gain in clarity and impact if presented in somewhat tighter form. But long, wretchedly organized books have been the tradition in Germany, and we may wonder whether a shorter, more lucid volume would have achieved the same reputation for profundity. In Germany, a book that is not hard to read is scarcely considered worth reading. As finally constituted, the German edition of the *Decline* runs to nearly twelve hundred pages and is full of repetitions of ideas, phrases, and, in one case, even of an entire paragraph. The sequence of thought is frequently difficult to grasp. Part of this difficulty is doubtless due to Spengler's highly personal method of writing. He composed his ideas originally in the form of aphorisms, which he kept in a portable trunk and left with friends whenever he went off on a journey. Many of his books—more particularly his later political works—started simply as collections of aphorisms.

Hence the lapidary, pictorial character of Spengler's writing. It is, as he himself noted in the preface to his revised first volume, "intuitive and depictive through and through, written in a language which seeks to present objects and relations illustratively instead of offering an army of ranked concepts. It addresses it-

---

[2] See the postscript by the editor, Dr. Hildegard Kornhardt, in Spengler's posthumously-published *Gedanken* (Munich, 1941), pp. 129–131.

self solely to readers who are capable of living themselves into the word-sounds and pictures as they read." [3] To others, trained in a smoother and more continuous style of exposition, the *Decline* may look like a disconnected series of massive, boldly-hewn segments of undifferentiated thought and deeply-colored imagery.

More closely regarded, however, Spengler's writing reveals its own characteristic logic. Its very repetitions and constant returns to familiar guiding principles begin to conform to a special sort of design. This pattern, Spengler subsequently complained, eluded nearly all his readers. They failed to grasp that thoughts like his could be conveyed only through examples, and that to fasten too literal-mindedly on any one of them meant to lose sight of its relation to the others. "For here everything hangs together so tightly that to take one particular point out of its context is already to fall into error." [4]

Hence even the back-trackings and repetitions play their part, indeed are nearly indispensable, in the tightly woven, all-interrelated effect that the author seeks to convey. Actually the *Decline* can hardly be said to start and end at any particular point. It is not to be read as a logical sequence. It is rather—to use the language of music to which Spengler was so deeply attracted —a theme and variations, a complex contrapuntal arrangement, in which no one idea necessarily follows another, but in which a group of ideas, whose mutual relationship is symbolically experienced rather than specifically understood, summon, answer, and balance one another in the sort of lofty cosmic harmony that Goethe's angels had proclaimed in the prologue and concluding stanzas of *Faust*.

*   *   *

Despite its length, the *Decline* failed to offer anything approaching an even coverage of the subject its author had undertaken to treat—the comparative morphology of culture. In conformity with what we have observed about Spengler's intellec-

[3] *Decline*, I, xiv.
[4] "Pessimismus?"; *Reden und Aufsätze*, p. 66.

tual preparation, he gave a full account only of those cultures with which he was reasonably well acquainted. Thus the *Decline* is primarily a series of comparisons between the attitudes of Western and classical man—and, to a lesser extent, that "Magian" man whom Spengler had sandwiched in between them. Three further cultures—the Egyptian, the Indian, and the Chinese— make their appearance at much rarer intervals. And two others —the Babylonian and the Mexican—figure hardly at all except in side references. To a final culture—the Russian—Spengler gave a rather special treatment, since he regarded it as a society whose true history had not yet begun.

Spengler's eventual roster of eight fully-developed cultures does not differ too widely, then, from Danilevsky's list of ten. Danilevsky's first four—the Egyptian, Chinese, Ancient Semitic, and Indian—reappear in practically identical form in the *Decline*. But the next five Spengler succeeds in reducing to two: he combines the Greek and Roman to make the classical or "Apollinian" culture, and Danilevsky's Iranian, Hebrew, and Arabian— plus some odd bits drawn from societies farther west—he fuses into his novel "Magian" concept. This leaves the Germano-Latin or European culture, to which Spengler's Western or "Faustian" closely corresponds. Significantly enough, the author of the *Decline* agrees with Danilevsky in placing Russia and Eastern Europe outside the sphere of what we usually call European society. Finally, of Danilevsky's two additional cultures that never reached maturity, one, the Mexican, Spengler promotes to full civilization status. The other, the Peruvian, he treats in a rather careless fashion. Although he mentions it at least once as having shared the fate of the culture of Mexico, he never elaborates, and we are left to presume that even Spengler's limitless industry stopped short of the effort required for an adequate understanding of Inca society.[5]

This, in fact, is the great, or at least the most obvious, trouble with the *Decline*. No man could possibly know or understand enough to write the work that Spengler had imagined. And

[5] *Decline*, II, 46.

so, when his knowledge proves insufficient, he is driven to desper-
ate expedients. He writes—as in connection with an obscure
epoch of Chinese history—that things *must* have happened in a
certain fashion.[6] Or, by a series of strained interpretations, he
stuffs his recalcitrant data willy-nilly into the pre-established
mould. At first all goes well. But the farther he gets from his central symbols the more difficult his task of universal harmonizing
becomes. Thus distinctions that have proved suitable and illuminating in the field of the plastic arts end up as forced and exag-
gerated when Spengler seeks to apply them to the more diffuse
data of political experience. In the end we may be dazzled—but
never totally convinced.

*   *   *

After an introductory flourish of mathematics (to which we
shall return in a moment), the *Decline* opens with the traditional
bow to metaphysics. Spengler's efforts in the realm of metaphysics
have met widely contrasting receptions inside Germany and
abroad. In Germany, a number of critics have taken them rather
more solemnly than they deserve. Elsewhere, they have encountered little but polite silence and occasional scorn. Especially in
the English-speaking countries, they have been tossed aside in
cavalier fashion as the indigestible bottom layer that necessarily
goes along with any of the heavier importations from Germany.
If only for this reason, Spengler's metaphysical musings deserve
our brief attention.

On the first page of his second volume, Spengler informed
his readers that for his more general reflections he was drawing
on a "metaphysical work" that he hoped "shortly to be able to
publish." [7] This hope never materialized. Of the vast study that
Spengler had projected, only fragments ever reached publication. In the meantime, what appeared in the *Decline* was not a
developed metaphysical system: it was rather a series of parallel
abstractions set one against another to explain Spengler's general
method of attack.

[6] *Ibid.*, II, 285.   [7] *Ibid.*, II, 3n.

Time versus space, existence versus consciousness, totem versus taboo—these contrasting sets of concepts, Spengler announces, exemplify our deepest, most nearly instinctive attitudes toward our universe. The former of each pair is more basic, more primitive, closer to the level of mere act. The second shows the beginning of the processes of thought, of what we call civilization. Concretely, these two attitudes find their earliest historical embodiment in the two original social classes—the nobility on the one side, the priesthood on the other. The former exemplifies what is dynamic, spontaneous, full of natural pride and passion. The latter strives for passionless understanding, and seeks to establish truths that will be valid for all time. In the architecture of castle and cathedral, their prime symbols confront each other in visible form.

Intellectualized, these same opposites appear in the contrast between history and natural science, destiny and causality, "physiognomic" and systematic comprehension. By now Spengler's own preference has become clear; he is solidly in the camp of the muscular as against the bloodless. The notion of destiny, he tells us, stands at the very center of his approach to history. "Destiny is a word whose content one *feels*. . . . Let no one believe that he has understood the kernel of my thinking if the ultimate meaning of this word, as *I* understand it, remains closed to him." "Destiny" is what operates in history, "cause" only in the natural sciences.

The present writer confesses that he is far from fully grasping the "ultimate meaning" of Spengler's word "destiny." Perhaps it is not necessary to do so. The notion of destiny, as Spengler uses it, obviously bears a close relation to the question of determinism in history that will occupy us again and again during this study. In more general terms, it represents Spengler's rather romantic way of protesting against one of the major tenets of positivism: the practice of assigning to historical movements and events, clear and determinable "causes," as in the natural sciences. The author of the *Decline,* like his more discerning contemporaries, saw that this procedure meant a ridiculous simplifi-

cation of the inextricable medley of converging elements that
went to make up even the least important item of history. Indeed,
when Spengler began to write, the inadequacy of such methods
had long been manifest. But while most twentieth-century historians went on to attempt a rational explanation—knowing full
well that their conclusions could be no more than the best among
a number of informed guesses—Spengler rejected the whole
notion of logical analysis. Such "systematic" practices, he tells
us, properly apply only in the natural sciences. To penetrate below the surface of history, to understand at least partially the
mysterious substructure of the past, a new method—that of
"physiognomic tact"—is required.

This new method, "which few people can really master,"
means "instinctively to see through the movement of events. It is
what unites the born statesman and the true historian, despite all
opposition between theory and practice." [8] It means the conscientious application of the lessons of Goethe and Nietzsche—of
the injunction to "sense" the reality of human events rather than
dissect them. In this new orientation, the historian ceases to be a
scientist and becomes a poet. He gives up the fruitless quest for
systematic understanding. By attempting the opposite, Spengler
argues, his predecessors got farther and farther off the track.
"The more historically men tried to think, the more they forgot
that in this domain they ought *not* to think." [9] They failed to
observe the most elementary rule of historical investigation:
respect for the *mystery* of human destiny.

Thus Spengler's pretentious metaphysic terminates in a clear
and quite sensible distinction between systematic and physiognomic method. Once we have grasped this distinction, our task
of analyzing his work becomes infinitely simplified. If we are still
somewhat uncertain as to what Spengler is trying to do, we at
least know what he is *not* trying to do. He is not writing the sort
of history that most of us have been trained to think of as the
only possible kind. Hence three-fourths of our objections simply

[8] "Pessimismus?"; *Reden und Aufsätze*, pp. 66–67.
[9] *Decline*, I, 96, 151.

fall to the ground as applicable to "systematic" history alone. All this may sound obvious, but few have paid any attention to it. Virtually none of Spengler's critics have taken the time to digest his statements on method. Fired by the discovery of some factual error, they have dashed off to meet him on a field of battle where he never had the slightest intention of putting in an appearance. Had the learned world read the *Decline* a little more carefully, the bulk of the great controversy might never have occurred.

* * *

The next step in a proper understanding of Spengler's theories is to review certain of his basic definitions. The words, the concepts that constantly recur in the *Decline* carry special meanings parcelled out by the author in fairly arbitrary fashion. To some of them—like the "Magian" culture—we have already been obliged to refer without adequate preliminary explanation.

First, there is the distinction between "culture" and "civilization"—originally invented by Nietzsche and later popularized by Thomas Mann in his influential First World War tract, *Reflections of an Unpolitical Man*. The former is the period of creative activity in a society, the latter the era of theoretical elaboration and material comfort. In the former, the "soul" of the countryside predominates, in the latter the "intellect" of the city. The former comprises the spring, summer, and autumn of a society, the latter its winter. Most civilizations continue hundreds, even thousands of years after their creativity is spent; China offers the classic example. Alone among recorded civilizations, the Roman world succumbed to outside pressure "in the moment of full splendour." [10] So long as the culture phase lasts, the leading figures in a society manifest a sure sense of artistic "style" and of personal "form." Indeed, the breakdown of style and form most clearly marks the transition from culture to civilization.

These cultures are mutually incomprehensible. The members of one culture cannot understand the basic ideas of another,

[10] *Ibid.,* II, 109.

and when they think they are doing so, they are actually trans-
lating totally alien concepts into concepts they have developed
on their own. Nor do cultures "influence" each other in any of
the usual senses of the term. What look like borrowings are simply the outer forms of art or public activity, into which the bor-
rowing culture has poured a new content. Obviously, Spengler is
unable to maintain this principle of water-tight compartments
with absolute rigor. To do so would be to deny the possibility of
making any significant statement about a culture other than one's
own. Spengler gets around this difficulty by implying—though
never in unequivocal terms—that for a handful of rare intuitive
spirits like himself, such comprehension is not totally unattainable. And since cultures follow parallel courses, it is both possible
and profitable to draw comparisons among them. In particular,
the historian may single out the comparable phenomena that
appear at comparable stages in the development of different cultures. Using an old term in a new sense, he may quite properly
refer to them as "contemporaneous."

Up to this point, the process of definition has gone along
relatively smoothly. But when Spengler comes to pinning down
certain of his concepts with greater precision, he gets into difficulties that his more cautious competitors have wisely avoided.
Two of his ideas in particular—the notion of fixed time sequences
and the concept of "pseudomorphosis"—have always figured in
the very center of the Spengler controversy.

On the question of time sequences, Spengler's position is not
quite so dogmatic as his critics have sometimes supposed. With
an unaccustomed modesty, he phrases his definition in the form
of a question:

What is the meaning of that striking fifty-year period, the
rhythm of the political, intellectual and artistic "becoming"
of all Cultures? Of the 300-year period of the Baroque, of
the Ionic, of the great mathematics, of Attic sculpture, of
mosaic painting, of counterpoint, of Galileian mechanics?
What does the *ideal* life of one millennium for each Culture

mean in comparison with the individual man's "three-score years and ten?" [11]

Each culture, then, is not limited to a definite span of a thousand years. The figure is merely "ideal," as with the seventy years of man, and may vary widely in either direction. Yet Spengler will not rest satisfied with this saving vagueness. He appends to his introduction three chronological charts showing the parallel development of spiritual, artistic, and political life in four different cultures. By thus concretizing his theory, Spengler weakens it. In the chronological tables, his regular time-spans take on a new rigidity. The gaps and ambiguities in his structure of comparisons show up naked and unadorned. In devising his tables, Spengler seems to have forgotten that the strength of his perspective on history lies in its imaginative imprecision. From this standpoint, the charts represent an obvious absurdity. In trying to force his vision into a mechanical and totally inappropriate pattern, Spengler falls victim to that very "systematic" method he has ostensibly rejected. He offers a broad and fair target for the mockery of his critics. In the conflict between Spengler the imaginative seer and Spengler the unwitting positivist, the charts represent a notable victory for the forces of "reaction." They convert the notion of cultural time-spans from a merely suggestive hypothesis into a fixed principle to be defended against all comers.

If the chronological charts represent a betrayal of Spengler's imaginative method, the concept of pseudomorphosis is, if anything, too imaginative. In recasting a whole series of categories dear to the specialists, it offers perhaps the most daring intellectual construction in the entire *Decline*. Spengler is only doing himself justice when he claims it as his personal "discovery."

After bobbing up at frequent intervals all through the earlier part of the book, the concept itself does not receive a full definition until nearly half way through the second volume:

By the term "historical pseudomorphosis" I propose to designate those cases in which an older alien Culture lies so

[11] *Ibid.*, I, 110.

massively over the land that a young Culture, born in this land, cannot get its breath and fails not only to achieve pure and specific expression-forms, but even to develop fully its own self-consciousness. All that wells up from the depths of the young soul is cast in the old moulds, young feelings stiffen in senile works, and instead of rearing itself up in its own creative power, it can only hate the distant power with a hate that grows to be monstrous.

This was the case in the decades just before the birth of Christ, "in the countries between Nile and Tigris, Black Sea and South Arabia," where the "Magian soul" awoke to life.[12] Everywhere the political power of Rome, the cultural prestige of Hellenism dominated the minds and activities of men. The new way of feeling could find expression only by twisting to fresh purposes the established forms of art and society. Thus, Spengler argues, in the first four centuries of our era, two ways of life existed side by side in overlapping territories: the "civilization" of the aging classical world, and the thwarted springtime of the new Magian culture. Most, in fact, of what the conventional histories have called "late Roman"—Neo-Platonic philosophy, the dome of the Pantheon, the government of Diocletian and Constantine—Spengler redefines as manifestations of the Magian spirit.

Yet the center of gravity of the new feeling lay in the eastern part of the empire, and it was in an area outside the control of Rome—in South Arabia—that the Magian spirit was eventually to find an entirely independent embodiment. Although Spengler describes as Magian even most Western achievements of the first millennium of our era, he defines the spirit of Magian culture in terms that a European would consider characteristically "eastern." To the most diverse historical creations of the eastern Mediterranean he ascribes an underlying spiritual unity. In Spengler's reorganization of history, the Byzantine Empire, the art of the Arabesque, the three great monotheistic religions—the Hebrew, the Mohammedan, and the Christianity of the early Church—all

[12] *Ibid.*, I, 183; II, 42, 189.

figure as the works of Magian man. And the final unification of the Magian world through the overlordship of Islam—and, along with it, the definitive break with the West—come, fittingly enough, at the moment when Europe itself has nearly finished its period of preparation and is about to undertake the creation of its own characteristic forms of cultural life.

Close to the Magian world in spirit and inheriting from Byzantium its primitive patterns of art and religion is another culture—the Russian—that has suffered under the distorting weight of pseudomorphosis. Yet the Russian case represents a slightly different form of pseudomorphosis from the Magian. In Eastern Europe, Spengler finds, there existed no aging civilization to crush and thwart the growth of a new culture. It was rather the prestige of a neighboring culture, the Western, still in the full vigor of creativity, that awoke to premature activity the slumbering Russian spirit. This was the legacy of Peter the Great, whose brutal work of Europeanization permanently distorted the course of Russian development. "And thus," Spengler concludes, "a nationality whose destiny should have been to live without a history for some generations still was forced into a false and artificial history that the soul of Old Russia was simply incapable of understanding." [13]

In viewing Russia as a nation of the future with a destiny separate from that of Western Europe, Spengler's theory closely parallels that of Danilevsky and the Slavophils. It is far more likely to find a sympathetic hearing today than it was at the time Spengler originally conceived it. Then most educated Europeans simply assumed that Russia belonged with the West. Today—with the Western world and Russia arrayed against each other in hostile coalitions—the same people would doubtless assume the very opposite. For this reason, the further discussion of Spengler's theory of Russian history should be postponed until we come to assess the present-day relevance of his predictions about our own society.

In general, the concept of pseudomorphosis has not proved

[13] *Ibid.,* II, 193.

popular with professional historians. It has alarmed them nearly as much as the unfortunate chronological charts. Thrown off by the obvious violence to "facts" that the construction of a Magian concept entails, they have failed to appreciate its suggestive possibilities and imaginative power. Here again the characteristic literal-mindedness of Spengler's critics has prevented them from accepting even in part the guidance and illumination that he can offer.

*   *   *

At last Spengler is ready to define his basic symbol. But not quite—before getting down to business, he cannot resist the temptation to dazzle his readers with one more intellectual *tour de force*. He wants to convince them beyond even the flicker of a doubt that the notion of eternal truth must be discarded utterly. And so he returns to his earliest intellectual interests and writes a chapter on mathematics. Even in this most abstract and eternal of intellectual activities, he tries to tell us, there are no truths that have been proved for all time. As Apollinian man invented geometry, Magian man algebra, and Faustian man the calculus, so from one to another there has been no real succession of knowledge. The Western mathematician has only *seemed* to learn from his predecessors in other cultures. He may teach to school-children the geometry of the ancients, but he cannot really believe in it. For to each culture, numbers mean a totally different thing: to classical man, they meant magnitude, to Western man, mere relation. Thus the whole history of Western mathematics *"consists of a long, secret and finally victorious battle against the notion of magnitude."* [14] Nothing less could satisfy the soul of Faustian man, whose deepest and most permanent endeavor has been a striving for infinity.

The notion of infinity offers the clue to what is coming next. The basic symbol, the key to the "master pattern," the theme on which the variations will be played, will be one of space:

A deep identity unites the awakening of the *soul,* its birth into clear existence in the name of a Culture, with the sud-

[14] *Ibid.,* I, 76.

den realization of distance and time, the *birth of its outer world* through the symbol of extension; and thenceforth this symbol is and remains the *prime symbol* of that life, imparting to it its specific style and the historical form in which it progressively actualizes its inward possibilities.[15]

If we can grasp, then, the concept of space characteristic of each culture, we shall be able to establish the spiritual orientation that permeates all its works.

"The Egyptian soul," Spengler tells us, "saw itself as moving down a narrow and inexorably-prescribed life-path to come at the end before the judges of the dead." Hence the most characteristic constructions of Egyptian architecture "are not 'buildings' but a path enclosed by mighty masonry. The reliefs and the paintings appear always as rows which with an impressive compulsion lead the beholder in a definite direction." For the Chinese too, life is a "way." "But whereas the Egyptian treads to the end a way that is prescribed for him with an inexorable necessity, the Chinese *wanders* through his world; consequently, he is conducted to his god or his ancestral tomb not by ravines of stone . . . but by friendly Nature herself. . . . This Culture is the only one in which the art of gardening is a grand religious art." And it is as a stroll through a garden—by "devious ways through doors, over bridges, round hills and walls"—that the Chinese envisions his life's pilgrimage.[16]

For Apollinian man, the essence of existence expressed itself as body and form. He confined his activities and speculations to the here and now and abhorred the idea of size and distance. What was small, circumscribed, clearly-delimited—the city-state, the temple enclosed by a colonnade, the ideal figures of geometry— alone appealed to the Apollinian. The free-standing nude statue, with its harmonious contours and untroubled gaze, symbolized in visible form the classical attitude of personal detachment and serene acceptance of an inscrutable destiny.

[15] *Ibid.,* I, 174.　　　　　　　[16] *Ibid.,* I, 188–190.

To the Magian, life appeared as a cave, bathed in an un-
earthly light whose rays could pierce but not dispel the surround-
ing darkness. Light and darkness: the contrast is crucial to the
Magian spirit. It expresses a radical dualism that pictured life as
an unremitting struggle between the forces of good and evil. In
this conflict, magic potency alone counted. The systematic reasoning of the Greeks and Romans was nothing but vanity. And
so to the logic and personal judgment prized by both the classical
and the Western world, the Magian opposed the idea of a supra-
logical and impersonal *consensus*. If God was one, so also the
community of the orthodox must be one in spirit and conviction.
"In the Magian world, consequently, the separation of politics
and religion is theoretically impossible and nonsensical." [17] On
this, imperial Roman and Jew, Mohammedan and Orthodox
Christian, saw exactly alike.

What the nude statue was to the Apollinian, the art of the
fugue has been to the Faustian world. Like his ideal prototype—
the hero of Marlowe and Goethe—Faustian man has lived in
eternal restlessness, and in longing for the unattainable. His is the
art of endless vistas and limitless spaces. It began with the sky-
ward striving of the medieval cathedrals, found a new outlet in
the perspective and color of Renaissance and seventeenth-century
painting, and ended as music, which alone spoke a language sufficiently abstract to convey a sense of spiritual infinity. In the succession of historical type-figures, Faustian man has been the
supreme individualist. To the undifferentiated antique statue and
the classical tragedy of typical situations, he has opposed the art
of the portrait and the drama of personal development. His world
he has seen as dynamic movement, where the Apollinian contem-
plated it in static repose. In the will to conquer distance Faustian
man has created his most eloquent symbols: the Copernican view
of the universe, the faith of the explorer, and the machines that
decade by decade have produced more and traveled faster than
even their inventors had considered possible.

[17] *Ibid.*, II, 243.

Having stated the basic theme of contrasting space concepts, Spengler proceeds to a series of detailed elaborations that occupy the greater part of his two volumes. First art and music—which show the closest, or at least the most easily demonstrable, relation to the prime symbols—then religion and philosophy, then natural science, and finally politics and economics, are subjected to the now familiar Spenglerian technique of structural regrouping. While the method remains identical, the results are far from uniform. In trying to fit all human phenomena into the same pre-established pattern, Spengler imposes on his prime symbols a weight that they simply cannot bear. Hence as we read on, we sense a kind of intellectual spread, a tendency for the data to escape and run off on their own independent journeys. The second volume becomes a catch-all for a disconcerting variety of special inquiries. Insensibly, it shifts over into the realm of political controversy in which Spengler was to play out the next phase of his intellectual activity.

Obviously it would be pointless to attempt to summarize the content of these elaborations. On the other hand, we can scarcely discuss in intelligible fashion the impact of Spengler's ideas unless we have explained what they are. Fortunately, the nature of the subsequent controversy helps to narrow the field. Among the public at least, and, to a lesser extent, in the learned world as well, it was what Spengler had to say about his own culture, the Faustian, that aroused admiration or bitter denial. His readers were far less interested in his theories, however novel or startling, about Egypt or Greece or China. Quite naturally, they felt a real personal concern only for the fate of their own society. If we outline, then, Spengler's interpretation of the course of Western history, with brief glances at the comparable movements of classical antiquity, we shall be offering both a concrete example of his method in action and an essential introduction to the controversy ahead.

For Spengler, Western history does not start, as in the schoolbooks, with the fall of Rome in 476. The first five centuries of "medieval" history he regards as a kind of twilight era, in which the memories of Apollinian civilization, the constantly present example of Magian forms, and the stirrings of a new indigenous spirit struggled for possession of the Western European soul. It was not until the tenth century that the Faustian culture was born. With the reform of the Papacy, the reestablishment of an imperial authority, the articulation of feudal society, and the emergence of Romanesque architecture, the new culture manifests itself in clear and vigorous form. Its focal point is Christianity—not the original Church of the Magian world but virtually a new religion in which the dynamic morality of personal atonement and the intensely human cult of the Mother of God have driven out the gentle, tranquil ethic of selfless fellowship with Jesus exemplified in the primitive sacrament of baptism. This driving, aspiring faith gives to the springtime of the Faustian spirit a quality of high tension. Like its prototype in the Apollinian culture, the Homeric era—and here Spengler echoes Vico—the European Middle Ages overflow with the excitement of passionate deeds and spiritual discovery.

After unfolding its full possibilities in the triumphs of Gothic architecture and the theological constructions of scholastics and mystics, the first phase of Faustian culture breaks down in internal contradictions. One of these is the so-called "Renaissance." As a purely negative effort to return to the spirit of classical antiquity, the Renaissance failed utterly; its greatest achievements proved to be Faustian in spite of themselves. The Renaissance was essentially an affair of the nobility. Its spiritual counterpart, the Reformation, represented an incomparably more important change in orientation for the other traditional social class, the clergy. For the Reformation remained faithful to the Gothic, the Faustian spirit. It could exert an influence that would be both positive and permanent. Most characteristically, the Reformation formed part of the shift in the cultural center of gravity from the countryside to the city that marked the end of Europe's youth. The Reformation was urban in origin and spirit. As a city phenomenon, it was to provide a religious foundation for a third social class, the new bourgeoisie. And it was to find a militant political embodiment in the figure of Cromwell—corresponding

to and "contemporary" with Pythagoras in the Apollinian world
and Mohammed in the Magian.

In the new society of the cities, Faustian culture was to reach
maturity, to experience its summer unfolding. The artistic embodiment of this ripe culture is the Baroque—actually a continuation
of the Gothic, whatever the art histories may say. As the architecture of the Baroque, in its striving for infinity, dissolves traditional
form and line into a fluid, bewildering succession of curves and
structural deceptions, so the great painters of the seventeenth
century push perspective and shadow to their farthest limits of
metaphysical depth. Ultimately the Faustian spirit has no recourse
but to take flight into the realm of music. From about 1670 on,
music dominates the cultural life of the West.

Intellectually, the era is one of free inquiry and scientific
speculation. Its characteristic thinker is Descartes—the philosophical "contemporary" of the pre-Socratics. Yet this intellectual
freedom is far from unlimited; it sets its own boundaries in acceptance of a rigorously-defined style of thought and in loyalty to
constituted authority. This authority—the political expression of
Faustian maturity—is the dynastic state. A régime based on
"estates," in which the king rules in understanding with the recognized social orders of the realm, the seventeenth-century monarchy represents a dynamic compromise, not a fixed and permanent political structure. The early part of the century witnesses its
first great crisis, a series of national "Frondes," in which the
nobles struggle for the restoration of their feudal privileges. In
alliance with the middle class, the kings put down the threat to
their authority. With the defeat of this "reactionary" revolution—
corresponding to the first wave of city-state tyrannies in the
ancient world—the monarchs of Europe are free to establish the
political absolutism that is to characterize the next century.

The eighteenth century is the autumn of the Faustian soul.
As such it bears a double aspect. On the one hand, it offers the
last and most exquisite creations of fully-realized style and form:
the perfection of diplomatic technique and aristocratic manners;
the art of the Rococo; the music of Mozart; the philosophical

writings of Kant and Goethe, who like Plato and Aristotle in the Apollinian world, give to the deepest speculations of their culture a conclusive formulation. As against this positive, creative aspect, the contrasting tendency of criticism and destruction comes more and more to predominate as the century advances. In the rationalism of the Enlightenment, the city reveals its ultimate sterility. Where earlier a host of cities, strongly differentiated and with an intense local consciousness, produced the most varied artistic and intellectual life, now a few great cities like Paris and London draw all aspiring talents into an ever-tightening circle. In these ultra-refined coteries, the conversation becomes recklessly critical, the old intellectual conventions are openly mocked. The century ends in revolution—the great revolution of 1789, in which the middle class, raised in the service of despotism to a knowledge of its own power, discards its former ally and assumes authority itself. In a futile attempt at self-preservation, the monarchy makes peace with its old enemies, the two traditional classes. Neither side, however, can claim the final victory: this goes to Napoleon —the "romantic" tyrant and "contemporary" of Alexander the Great.

With the nineteenth century begins the winter of the West, the "civilization" phase of the Faustian spirit. Its thousand (in this case nine hundred) years of "culture" have passed, and there is no creativity left in it. As opposed to the instinctive sense for form and style that characterized preceding centuries, the new age is inchoate and uncertain. This formlessness reflects the hostility of the now dominant middle classes to the aristocratic virtues of refined manners and sure taste, and their temperamental yearning for untrammeled freedom. Culturally it manifests itself in sharp and meaningless fluctuations of style: the warfare of classicism and Romanticism is followed by a succession of eclectic experiments. In philosophy, ethics displaces metaphysics, as a galaxy of "late" cults vie for public favor: the popular preachers of materialism and scepticism are to the nineteenth century what the Cynics and Epicureans were to antiquity. Socialism—a philosophy of resignation—performs the same function of ethical transvaluation as Stoicism in the Apollinian world and Buddhism in China. Equally meaningless are the forms of political life. The most characteristic of them, parliamentarism, is nothing more than a transition device, serving to obscure with hollow rhetoric the basic political reality—the triumph of money. Before the power of financial speculation, everything else must give way: constitutionalism, democracy, even socialism. Politicians have no choice but to become the paid agents of the financiers.

Yet their power is not eternal. With the twentieth century a new aspect of Faustian civilization is at length revealing itself. "Blood"—the world of pride and instinct—is about to regain its rights against the overlordship of money and intellect. A sudden upsurge of colonial imperialism has heralded the change, and imperialism in its widest sense will be the distinctive mark of the coming era. For an age of great wars is opening. This phase, which regularly occupies at least the first two centuries of each "civilization," has actually been in progress ever since the time of Napoleon. But the peculiar circumstances of the nineteenth century, in which the great powers, although always ready for war, never dared unleash a general conflict, have obscured the underlying realities. Now, with the World War of 1914–1918, it should be apparent to all that an era of nearly perpetual warfare has begun. These new conflicts, however, will differ radically from their predecessors. As opposed to the old wars between national armies, they will be the battles of personal followings, grouped around born leaders of rare military and political talent —the new Caesars. For Caesarism—the true world tyranny after the showy and transitory dress-rehearsals of an Alexander or a Napoleon—will be the guiding phenomenon of the new age. With their devoted bands of armed followers, the Caesars will struggle for the mastery of the world, while the mass of mankind will look on in bewilderment, apathy, or resignation, ready to accept without question the fate that a handful of victorious soldiers will impose. Eventually one of the Caesars will win out over all his rivals and establish a universal imperium.

Long before that time, political ideologies and parties will have lost any semblance of meaning. Life will have descended to a level of general uniformity, in which local and national differences will have virtually ceased to exist. The only places that will matter will be a handful of world cities—the "megalopolis," like New York or Berlin, as opposed to the eighteenth-century city of culture, which still retained some connection with a living tradition. These "barrack-cities" will be what Hellenistic Alexandria and imperial Rome were to the ancient world—vast assemblages of people living all on top of each other, a shiftless mob, willing to obey any leader who will keep them amused. Their life will be a meaningless repetition of purely mechanical tasks and vulgar, brutal diversions. Even intellectual activity will have become mechanized, practical, cold, and merely "clever." The educated will have lost their feeling for language, and the same "basic" speech—what Toynbee would call a "lingua franca"—will be on the lips of intellectuals and common laborers alike.

Eventually, when every trace of form and style will have disappeared, a new primitivism will begin to pervade all human activity. Even the feeling for scientific norms—which will have survived the dissolution of culture—will grow vague and uncertain. Men will be ready to believe anything; they will regain their appetite for the mysterious and the supernatural. In vulgar credulity, they will find an escape from the universal drabness and mechanization. Out of the desolation of the cities there will arise a "second religiosity," a fusion of popular cults and the memories of nearly forgotten piety. The patient, uncomprehending masses will have found a solace for their miseries.

* * *

In this new interpretation of Western history, the earlier part was far less original than what followed. Much of what Spengler had to say about the centuries from 900 to 1800 did not differ too markedly from the statements in the conventional histories. His springtime of the Faustian spirit looks very much like what is usually called the high Middle Ages, and his summer and autumn resemble the conventionally-delimited era of absolutism

and the Baroque. Even his beginning of the "civilization" phase
follows fairly closely the more generally accepted interpretation:
the French Revolution and Napoleon are commonly regarded as
having marked a decisive turning-point in history, and the standard manuals regularly describe the nineteenth century as a period
of artistic and intellectual eclecticism and of materialistic and
sceptical philosophies. It was not until he got to the twentieth
century that Spengler revealed the truly original implications of
his morphological method, and it was his account of his own time
and his predictions for the decades to come that chiefly shocked
and alarmed his readers.

Two things in particular upset them: the determinism of his
philosophical approach and the pessimism of his conclusions. On
the first of these points, Spengler had left little room for apology
or mitigation. In the introduction to the *Decline*, he had defined
his position in uncompromising terms. Every event of the present,
he had told his readers, was simply "the prelude of a future . . .
with which the history of West-European mankind will be definitely *closed*."

He who does not understand that this outcome is obliga-
tory and insusceptible of modification, that our choice is between willing *this* and willing nothing at all, between cleaving
to *this* destiny or despairing of the future and of life itself; he
who cannot feel that there is grandeur also in the realizations
of powerful intelligences, in the energy and discipline of
metal-hard natures, in battles fought with the coldest and
most abstract means; he who is obsessed with the idealism of
a provincial and would pursue the ways of life of past ages
—must forego all desire to comprehend history, to live
through history or to make history.

We cannot choose our destiny, Spengler tells us, and we have no
alternative but to make the best of the historical situation in
which we have been placed. But within the established master-
plan, there is still room for individual initiative. "Every situation
has its elastic limit," which it is the statesman's task to estimate

with rigorous accuracy. The "themes" are given, but their "modulations"—the precise fashion in which predetermined developments will play themselves out in the actual performance of history—depend on the character and capacities of the individual players. Nineteenth-century Germany could not fail to be united. But it was the personality of King Frederick William IV in 1848, and of Bismarck in 1870, that determined exactly how the unification should be accomplished.[18]

This concession of a minimum of freedom in the course of events limits the range of Spengler's pessimism. We need be pessimists, he assures us, only if we refuse to see the possibilities still open to us. In defending his own work three years after its original publication, Spengler accepted his critics' charge. "In what concerns the 'goal of mankind,' " he wrote, "I am a thorough and decided pessimist. For me mankind is a zoological quantity. I see no progress, no goal, no path for humanity." But a few paragraphs later he voiced an indignant denial: "No, I am not a pessimist. Pessimism means to see no more tasks. I see so many still unaccomplished that I fear we shall lack the time and men they demand." [19] The two statements are not incompatible. For Spengler, the term pessimism applies only to long-range philosophy: as a man of the present, he calls for action.

Hence the author of the *Decline* could conscientiously defend himself against the charge of discouraging and demoralizing his readers. Far from doing anything of the sort, he argued, he was rendering them a great service:

We are civilized, not Gothic or Rococo, people; we have to reckon with the hard cold facts of a *late* life, to which the parallel is to be found not in Pericles's Athens but in Caesar's Rome. Of great painting or great music there can no longer be, for Western people, any question. Their architectural possibilities have been exhausted these hundred years. Only *extensive* possibilities are left to them. Yet, for a

[18] *Ibid.*, I, 38, 145; II, 446.
[19] "Pessimismus?"; *Reden und Aufsätze*, pp. 73–75.

sound and vigorous generation that is filled with unlimited
hopes, I fail to see that it is any disadvantage to discover
betimes that some of these hopes must come to nothing. . . .
The lesson, I think, would be of benefit to the coming generations, as showing them what is possible—and therefore
necessary—and what is excluded from the inward potentialities of their time. Hitherto an incredible total of intellect
and power has been squandered in false directions. . . . And
I can only hope that men of the new generation may be
moved by this book to devote themselves to technics instead
of lyrics, the sea instead of the paint-brush, and politics instead of epistemology. Better they could not do.[20]

This philosophic advice—as the subsequent controversy was to
prove—the bulk of Spengler's readers simply refused to accept.

[20] *Decline*, I, 40–41.

CHAPTER SIX

THE CONTROVERSY: FROM GERMANY TO THE UNITED STATES

NINETEEN-NINETEEN was the "Spengler year." Everyone seemed to be reading him; everyone was wondering just who he was. "Never had a thick philosophical work had such a success—and in all reading circles, learned and uneducated, serious and snobbish." [1] Within eight years after the original publication, total sales had reached a hundred thousand. Spengler, like Schopenhauer and Nietzsche before him, had become the philosopher of the hour.

Among the general public, the entirely accidental circumstance that the appearance of the *Decline* coincided with Germany's military defeat was the decisive element in the initial reaction. This was the reason why Spengler's readers fastened on his pessimism to the neglect of his more positive pronouncements. Quite understandably, the *Decline* appealed to people who were frantically seeking rationalizations for the despair they already felt. And to Germans nursing the humiliation of defeat, it was comforting to learn that their late enemies were actually no better off than themselves; no Western nation, Spengler had taught them, could escape the universal verdict of doom. In thus consoling themselves, of course, Spengler's readers conveniently forgot that the "decline" in question was rather a slow sinking than a sudden catastrophe. But such intellectual refinements were only for more careful students of the book. For the run of post-war

[1] Quoted from W. Wolfradt in Manfred Schroeter, *Der Streit um Spengler: Kritik seiner Kritiker* (Munich, 1922), p. 7n.

Germans, the peculiar circumstances of defeat and revolution had actually raised pessimism to the status of a popular doctrine.

It was rather the scholars and the specialists who objected to Spengler's gloomy predictions. The hubbub of the initial popular enthusiasm had scarcely quieted down, when the learned world began to bring to bear on the rash intruder its heaviest artillery. "The official philosophers reproached him with shallowness, the official specialists with incompetence and charlatanism." [2] Virtually all of them—young and old, conservative and leftist—recoiled from the notion of a predetermined future. In a half-instinctive movement of self-defense, they rejected the thesis of inevitable decline—"as though a deep and secret wound had been grievously probed" by a clumsy hand.[3]

Among the hundreds of articles and reviews that combed over every aspect of the *Decline,* very few found any virtue in it. Of the theologians a certain number were favorable, seeing in Spengler's pessimism a kind of springboard for a revival of Christianity—and thereby revealing that they quite thoroughly misunderstood his idea of a "second religiosity." Most, however, found in the *Decline* an irreligious absolutism masked under an ostensible relativism. The historians of art and of music were sharply divided. While the former objected to Spengler's rigid lines of demarcation between cultures, the latter expressed pleasure that someone should at length have given music its proper place as the focal point of Western creativity. Most surprising of all, perhaps, was the verdict of Ulrich von Wilamowitz, the terrible old man of classical scholarship. Half a century before he had demolished Nietzsche's *Birth of Tragedy* with the celebrated phrase: "This work does not exist for science." By 1921, he had mellowed sufficiently to grant that Spengler's "schematic constructions," while "unhistorical," were distinctly "ingenious." [4]

[2] Theodor W. Adorno, "Spengler nach dem Untergang: Zu Oswald Spenglers 70. Geburtstag," *Der Monat,* 2. Jahrgang, May 1950, p. 115.

[3] Schroeter, *op. cit.,* p. 13.

[4] Ulrich von Wilamowitz-Möllendorff, "Die Geltung des klassischen Altertums im Wandel der Zeiten," *Velhagen & Klasings Monatshefte,* 36. Jahrgang, 1. Heft, September 1921, p. 76.

It was the professional historians who were most nearly united in their condemnation of the *Decline*. Both idealists and positivists, for contrasting reasons, were incensed by Spengler's claim to superior knowledge. The latter, quite predictably, refused to accept his separation of history from nature, of the realm of "destiny" from the realm of causality. Speaking for his positivist colleagues, Erich Brandenburg, the historian of German unification, rose to the defense of history as a science. Spengler's intuitive method, he maintained, was nothing more than a "wild, reckless, uncontrolled construction of hypotheses." The author of the *Decline* was suffering from a "mighty self-deception" if he thought he could draw on a "peculiar source of knowledge" of his own, having "nothing to do with science and superior to it." By accepting intuition as a "higher organ of perception," Brandenburg concluded, Spengler's scepticism had "transformed itself . . . into a dogmatism resting on a foundation of pure feeling." [5]

The controversy attained its climax with the publication of a special number of the review *Logos,* in which seven specialists, each from the standpoint of his own discipline, did their best to submerge the *Decline* in a flood of erudition. This time the scholars had over-reached themselves. The introduction to the series provoked considerable mirth by the scolding tone in which it warned its readers against the dangerous effects of Spengler's book, and the seven articles were too chopped-up to meet any of the major issues on a sufficiently broad front. This, in general, had been the trouble with the whole controversy. Nearly all of Spengler's critics had attacked him only on narrow and pedantic grounds—or from the standpoint of a "healthy optimism." The way was wide open for Spengler to counter-attack with the full force of his highly-charged rhetoric.

Such was the purpose of the article "Pessimism?" that appeared in the spring of 1921. In it Spengler complained that his readers had almost invariably misunderstood what he was trying to say. He regretted that they had paid insufficient attention to his

[5] Erich Brandenburg, "Spenglers 'Untergang des Abendlandes,'" *Historische Vierteljahrschrift,* XX, 1. Heft, 1920, pp. 18, 21.

political writings, which had begun to appear a year and a half before and which contained the "ethical" ideas that were to be more fully developed in the second volume of the *Decline*. In concentrating on the negative side of his theories, Spengler noted, his readers had been led astray by the title of his book. They had gotten the impression that his notion of decline was something like that of the sinking (*Untergang*) of an ocean liner. He had originally chosen his title to combat the "trivial optimism" of the pre-war years—to point up the "aspect of historical development . . . that nobody at that time was willing to see." Had he to choose again, he would "try to combat with another formula the equally trivial pessimism" of the post-war era.

Hence few had recognized the "active" intention of his work. Most people had not realized that "every line not written to serve active living" seemed to Spengler "superfluous." Only occasional readers—like certain Germans in America—had written to him that the *Decline* had worked as a powerful source of inspiration on those "resolved to *be* something in life." [6]

"Pessimism?" did little to enhance Spengler's reputation. It was too violent, too intransigent to win over the critics who had already taken up positions against him. And in arguing so strongly for an activist philosophy of life, it represented a betrayal of what was permanently valuable in the *Decline*. In reinterpreting his own book as primarily a work of political controversy, Spengler had simply revealed the direction in which his own intellectual interests were shifting. He had made of the *Decline* a lesser thing than it really was. But as a work of clarification "Pessimism?" was not a total failure. By raising the controversy to a plane of intellectual generalization, it prepared the way for two critics who were qualified to present Spengler's case far better than he could ever have argued it himself.

The first of these was Manfred Schroeter, whose remarkable little book, *The Spengler Controversy*, was published in 1922, just after the second volume of the *Decline*. Originally one of Spengler's critics, Schroeter had been increasingly impressed by

[6] "Pessimismus?"; *Reden und Aufsätze*, pp. 63–64, 73–74.

the "demoniacal strength" of his writing. The *Decline*, he had become convinced, was a phenomenon of "definite significance for the cultural consciousness of the present time." It should be viewed from a loftier standpoint than Spengler's scholarly critics had to date cared to adopt. As an introduction to this higher understanding, Schroeter offered a conscientious catalogue of all the arguments, major and minor, that had gone into the controversy. Virtually all of them, he found, had missed the essential point—that Spengler belonged to the handful of German writers since Nietzsche who had tried to understand the contemporary scene in all its depth and complexity. Where the professional historians had shirked the task, it had been left to men like Spengler —or like Thomas Mann and Arthur Moeller van den Bruck, the visionary author of *The Third Reich*—to catch the essential quality of the present in flashes of inspired understanding. "Whoever does not feel, behind Spengler's violent constructions, the breath of a mighty, incomparably alive understanding of culture, will never be able to get beyond mere negative objections." [7]

Both the scientific and the intuitive approach, Schroeter argued, were necessary to the understanding of history. And it was in his immediate intuitions that Spengler's real strength lay— not in the complicated, frequently mistaken structure he built over them. Such elaborations simply made for further misunderstandings between the scientific and intuitive methods. Moreover, Spengler's critics were quite wrong in fearing the infection of his ideas. These were too personal a construction to attract a circle of "Spenglerians." The conclusion doubtless seemed paradoxical at the time. But the subsequent vicissitudes of the *Decline* were to confirm it.

Two years later, a professional historian was at length ready to come to Spengler's defense. In a brief but comprehensive address before the German Historical Congress of 1924, Eduard Meyer, a historian of antiquity for whom the author of the *Decline* had a high regard, gave his qualified approval to Spengler's two major theses. Both the comparative method of cultural

[7] Schroeter, *op. cit.*, pp. iv, 2–4, 36.

study and the view of the present as a time of artistic and institutional decline, Meyer found justified by the course of history. "Consciously or unconsciously," he wrote, "we are all oppressed by the feeling that we are decadents." [8] Yet to many of Spengler's subsidiary theories Meyer objected strongly. He refused to accept the more dogmatic assertions in the *Decline*—the unitary view of each culture, the virtual denial of cultural interaction, and the failure to distinguish between cultures growing up in isolation and those deriving from pre-existing civilizations. The "Magian" concept he rejected as a difficult and amorphous construction, spread out in time and space. Nor did he agree with Spengler's treatment of the history of Greece and Rome as the record of a single culture. And in its analysis of Faustian society, he found that the *Decline* had overlooked the importance of national differences. All these specific criticisms, however, Meyer relegated to a secondary position. It was only in its overwhelming totality that he was willing to judge the significance of Spengler's work.

Both in the breadth of its viewpoint and in the date of its delivery, Meyer's address closed the Spengler controversy. As early as 1920 the general public had begun to lose interest, and by 1924 even the scholarly furor had largely subsided. The German public—driven to distraction by a galloping inflation and endemic civil war—had turned to more immediate and practical concerns.

*   *   *

In the meantime the rest of the "Faustian" world had begun to show an interest in Spengler's theories. Abroad such interest was originally far less intense than in Germany, and most of the press notices were comparatively superficial in tone. This was even true of the august Croce, who airily dismissed the *Decline* as a mere repetition of what Vico had said two centuries before.[9] Once the oracle of historical idealism had spoken, a host of dis-

---

[8] Eduard Meyer, *Spenglers Untergang des Abendlandes* (Berlin, 1925), p. 3.
[9] Benedetto Croce, "Il tramonto dell'Occidente," *La Critica,* XVIII, 1919; reprinted in *Pagine sulla Guerra,* seconda edizione (Bari, 1928), pp. 312–317.

ciples—particularly in Italy, where Croce ruled as the near-dictator of intellectual life—were ready to fall in behind him.

The French quite predictably received the *Decline* with mocking scorn. Nothing could have been more alien to the Gallic tradition of logical analysis and precise definition. Typical was the retrospective verdict of Lucien Febvre:

> In the twenties Spengler offered the wares that at that time were most in demand: a certain pathos, a determined anti-intellectualism, a heroic notion of destiny, anti-aestheticism, the thrill of the mere human being before the majesty, the broad majesty, of History. . . . This is what gave Spengler his success: not the success of an analytical and deductive historian, but the success of a prophet, of a magician, of a visionary perfectly adapted to the needs of a troubled Germany. . . .[10]

This connection between Spengler's teachings and the demands of a "troubled Germany" was something that the French could not fail to notice. Even those who recognized the imaginative power of the *Decline* were disturbed by its political implications. Thus André Fauconnet, the most conscientious of Spengler's French critics, at the end of a comparatively sympathetic analysis of the *Decline,* warned his readers that Spengler's political ideas were "fighting slogans simple and clear enough to become some day the credo of a great popular party passionately devoted to imperialism and state socialism." [11]

In England the *Decline* received a "cool but not unsympathetic reception." [12] It was introduced in authoritative fashion to the general public by the historian G. P. Gooch, who in a widely-read study of the post-war Reich, referred to it as "the most important and influential work published in Germany during the last decade." [13] Typical of the more unfavorable comments were

[10] Lucien Febvre, "De Spengler à Toynbee: Quelques Philosophies opportunistes de l'Histoire," *Revue de Métaphysique et de Morale,* 43° Année, N° 4, October 1936, p. 579.

[11] Fauconnet, *op. cit.,* p. 136.   [12] Schroeter, *op. cit.,* p. 9*n.*

[13] G. P. Gooch, *Germany* (London, 1925), p. 329.

two analytical articles by R. G. Collingwood, which with uncompromising logic dissected the whole notion of historical cycles.[14]
On the other side of the controversy there appeared a confessed
popularization of Spengler's theories, *Civilisation or Civilisations,*
by E. H. Goddard and P. A. Gibbons.[15] The latter two studies
were both published in the second half of the 1920's, and in general the reaction to Spengler in English-speaking countries came
later than on the Continent. But this very delay seems to have
given the *Decline* a more permanent popularity—at least in
America—than it was able to hold in the countries where it had
originally appeared.

For of all areas outside Germany it was the New World that
proved most enthusiastic about Spengler's doctrines. In Argen-
tina, Professor Ernesto Quesada wrote a highly laudatory philosophical analysis of the *Decline,* and in the United States, after a
slow start, Spengler's work won an increasing number of con-
verts. Here, as elsewhere, the scholarly world was unimpressed.
Speaking for the vast majority of his colleagues in political science and history, Professor James T. Shotwell rejected Spengler's
whole historical construction. The author of the *Decline,* Shotwell maintained, had failed to recognize that scientific progress
had made Western civilization more resistant to internal seepage
than any of its predecessors. Its potentialities for the development
of "democracy" and "justice" were far from exhausted.[16] Shotwell's argument added little to the Spengler debate. In intellectual
sophistication it remained on the level of the original controversy.
Science and temperamental optimism—in the United States as in
Germany these twin vestiges of the nineteenth-century credo were
to continue to bar the way to an understanding of the more subtle
aspects of Spengler's thought.

[14] R. G. Collingwood, "Oswald Spengler and the Theory of Historical
Cycles," *Antiquity: a Quarterly Review of Archaeology,* I, September 1927, pp.
311–325; "The Theory of Historical Cycles: II. Cycles and Progress," *Ibid.,*
December 1927, pp. 435–446.

[15] E. H. Goddard and P. A. Gibbons, *Civilisation or Civilisations: An Essay
in the Spenglerian Philosophy of History* (London, 1926).

[16] James T. Shotwell, "Spengler," in *Essays in Intellectual History Dedicated to James Harvey Robinson* (New York, 1929), pp. 55–67.

In the late 1920's, with the publication of an English translation, the *Decline* began to reach the American public. In 1926, Alfred A. Knopf brought out the first volume of Charles Francis Atkinson's faithful and scholarly version. Two years later, the second volume followed. From the start sales were steady although never spectacular. By 1940, the total had reached twenty-one thousand—plus five thousand of the first volume alone. And in the late 1920's and early 1930's Spengler's theories had become a fashionable topic for semi-intellectual conversation.[17] They admirably fitted the prevailing temper of a rather callow scepticism.

Elsewhere the *Decline* was translated into French, Spanish, Italian, Russian, and Arabic. In many lands the public was reacting with characteristic stubbornness against the boycott imposed by the men of learning. Most of these readers, however, knew Spengler simply as the philosopher of inevitable decline. They had not heard of his later writings and they tended to gloss over the political implications of his historical work. Had they read his subsequent political utterances, many of the more gentle Spenglerians, particularly in the United States, would doubtless have quickly repudiated their intellectual idol.

[17] As a reflection of this mood, and an answer to it, see the youthful work of William Harlan Hale, *Challenge to Defeat: Modern Man in Goethe's World and Spengler's Century* (New York, 1932).

CHAPTER SEVEN

THE TWENTIES:
THE POLITICAL PHASE

T O most of his readers, Spengler was a man of mystery. He lived an extremely retired life, he had few friends, and he belonged neither to the regular academic profession nor to any recognized literary circle. To what extent this obscurity was a matter of conscious choice, or merely a rationalization of a situation beyond his control, it would be difficult to say. Certainly, if he had wished to enter into more frequent relations with the outside world, he would have had trouble in finding a suitable niche in a country like Germany—where even bohemians were in the habit of attaching themselves to some regularly constituted artistic movement. He had cut himself off from the profession of secondary-school teaching, and his writing was too unorthodox and his temperament too independent to fit him for the average university post. It is true that a few months after the first appearance of the *Decline* he had been informally approached about a chair of philosophy at the University of Göttingen. But he had refused the suggestion, alleging his lack of competence for specialized teaching and the late start he had made in his chosen field, which now necessitated a total concentration on his projected writings. Fourteen years later, he was to take the same attitude toward his only formal university offer—a professorship at Leipzig once held by the well-known historian Karl Lamprecht.

Nor was Spengler enough of a literary figure to become a

98

major influence in a Germany where the lesser lights almost by necessity gravitated toward such leading writers as Rainer Maria Rilke, Stefan George, and Thomas Mann. For a while he showed a certain interest in the George circle—whose cult of Nietzsche paralleled his own—but he never tried to get in contact with it. Temperamentally he was unfitted to play the role of a faithful adherent of a coterie. Both personal inclination and practical necessity dictated an attitude of proud independence. Despite his fame, Spengler had chosen to live as a lonely and isolated figure —a "Faustian" to the end.

In the latter part of the year 1919 Spengler's financial position began to improve. He was able to move to much better quarters—a large apartment in the Widenmayerstrasse overlooking the Isar river. An American visitor has described it as a "vast expanse of room, mostly library, with three large windows facing the Isar, a wide entrance hall, and a long expanse of Turkey-red carpet." The carpet, Spengler explained, was "something he had always wanted," which the returns from the *Decline* had at length permitted him to buy; pacing up and down on it was the way "he did all of his thinking, worked out his problems." On the walls were "paintings by minor Italian masters," which Spengler "took great joy in collecting." In this apartment, the author of the *Decline* lived the life of a studious bachelor. Of regular visitors we know only of August Albers, a "confidential clerk" who worked with Spengler's publishers and "was the learned man's devoted slave." [1] Deeply impressed by his reading of the *Decline*, Albers had written to its author, then paid him a visit, and subsequently had seen him at least as often as once a week. It was in "countless walks" with Albers that Spengler had thought out loud the contents of his second volume.[2] Of other intimate contacts there were apparently only Spengler's two sisters, still in the Harz, whom he occasionally went to visit.

[1] Recollections of Alfred A. and Blanche Knopf, in the biographical note appended to Edwin Franden Dakin's *Today and Destiny: Vital Excerpts from the Decline of the West of Oswald Spengler* (New York, 1940), pp. 358–359.
[2] Albers, *op. cit.*, p. 129.

Further knowledge of his character can be deduced from fragmentary reminiscences of his personal habits. From these we learn of his "pleasure in long walks and mountain-climbing; his delight in talking with peasants, before whom he lost his austerity; his refusal to call doctors for fevers that sent others to bed." [3] His household was well-ordered, and his interests were natural and simple. For both Blankenburg, his birthplace, and Munich, his adopted home, he had a kind of traditional loyalty. He used to tell humorous stories about the people of the Harz and he enjoyed learning the local traditions of his Bavarian fellow-citizens. A heavy eater and a beer-drinker, Spengler was a habitué of the Franziskaner beer cellar, where he was well acquainted with its rather popular clientele.

The first thing that struck visitors in Spengler's personal appearance was his "vast forehead and bald dome." He seemed "enormous in bulk, very forceful-looking." Always quietly dressed, he was a "soft-spoken man with a pleasant, kindly voice, . . . agreeable, friendly, and interesting, . . . human and considerate." [4] But this impression of benevolence is somewhat belied by his literary style and by the face that looks out at us from his photographs. In this tense, forbidding countenance we find the same expression of anger and indomitable resolve that emerges from his writing. Irritability and self-mastery seem to be struggling for the upper hand. The troubled gaze reflects that uneasy combination of harshness and sensitivity that has so often marked the German intellectual.

*   *   *

The half decade following the original publication of the *Decline* was Spengler's period of fame. And it was in these five years that he made his bid for political influence. The situation in Germany lent itself to such activity. The military defeat, the establishment of a republic, had brought no stability or basic agreement on the nation's constitution and political future. While the

[3] Dakin, *op. cit.*, biographical note, pp. 354–355.
[4] Recollections of the Knopfs, *Ibid.*, pp. 358–359.

moderate parliamentary parties were ostensibly in control, they commanded little support among the more influential leaders of public opinion. These took their stand either on the left or on the right of the governing coalition: on the one side, Communists and Independent Socialists pressed for the true revolution that had somehow misfired; on the other side, monarchists, traditional nationalists, and the new enthusiasts of racism and direct action demanded the restoration of a hierarchical society and the refurbishing of the "national honor." Both sides were quite ready to take up arms when a suitable occasion offered: city streets and countryside witnessed regular battles between revolutionary Marxists and adherents of the Free Corps, the semi-legal military formations of war veterans and nationalistically-minded students. In such a fluid situation, the field was wide open for German intellectuals to find a hearing. And the early twenties became a period of intense competition among the most varied gospels of political and moral regeneration.

In this intellectual jockeying for position, Spengler clearly aligned himself with the conservatives. But his conservatism was far from orthodox. Convinced as he was that the traditional ruling classes of Germany had let their country down by leading it into a disastrous war, Spengler sought a new basis of social cohesion. In this search, his efforts paralleled and occasionally linked up with the work of such writers as Walther Rathenau, Thomas Mann, and Arthur Moeller van den Bruck. All were groping for a new moral foundation for German conservatism; all were striving for a resolution of class conflict in some working formula for national harmony. Most frequently they found it in corporatism —the doctrine that a frank recognition of class interests and their formal incorporation into the structure of government could alone lead to their reconciliation.[5]

It is somewhat difficult to decide with which of Spengler's political writings to begin. The first in date of publication was the

[5] On this whole subject, see Klemens von Klemperer, *Germany's New Conservatism: Its History and Dilemma in the Twentieth Century* (Princeton, 1957), and Fritz Stern, *The Politics of Cultural Despair: A Study in the Rise of the Germanic Ideology* (Berkeley and Los Angeles, 1961).

little book *Prussianism and Socialism,* which appeared in 1919—
that is, between the first and second volumes of the *Decline.* On
the other hand, the large chapter on the state, which formed the
core of the second volume, was probably the earlier of the two in
conception. We have seen that it was the outgrowth of that work
of political theory which the *Decline* was originally intended to
be. For this reason, and because the chapter on the state gives
Spengler's political ideas in their most abstract and generalized
form, it seems best to start with what is technically the later work.

At the center of Spengler's political theory is the notion of
social class—or, more properly, of estates. We have observed
earlier that Spengler regarded the two original estates—nobility
and priesthood—as immediate manifestations of a basic metaphysical opposition. In them, the cultural values of "form" and
"style" can alone find meaningful and dignified expression. The
advent of a third estate—the urban bourgeoisie—with its individualist and anti-symbolic attitude toward life, is already a pre-
monition of decline. And with the fourth estate—the masses—
the rejection of culture becomes total; the masses are formless by
definition. Hence for Spengler democracy, far from being a political blessing, is a prime agent in the destruction of cultural values.
A functioning democracy is an impossibility: what naive enthusiasts call democracy is no more than a chaotic transition regime—
a temporary halt on the road to Caesarism.

For, in Spengler's view, all real government must by necessity be aristocratic. "Class-States—that is, States in which particular classes rule—are the *only* States. . . . *Every nation is represented in history by a minority.* . . . Politically gifted *peoples* do
not exist. Those which are supposed to be so are simply peoples
that are firmly in the hands of a ruling minority and in consequence feel themselves to be in good form." Hence a well-run
state is almost by necessity one in which an estate of nobles—with
or without legal recognition—plays the leading role. For among
the nobility alone are those virtues systematically cultivated which
are essential to statecraft—"unforced unity of . . . impulse, diplo-
macy, judgment of men, the art of command and masculine will

to keep and extend power, . . . the feeling for honour and brav-
ery." [6] And—in Western Europe at least—aristocratic rule has
best found expression through the institutions of a dynastic
monarchy.

If this is the reality of politics, then political ideologies are
essentially meaningless. They are merely slogans. "In the world of
facts, truths are simply *means,* effective in so far as they dominate
spirits and therefore determine actions. . . . But, *as* catchwords,
they are for about two centuries powers of the first rank." The
question of whether they are "deep, correct, or even merely logical," is quite unimportant. Their practical effectiveness alone
counts. Hence the slogan that eventually wins has in the verdict
of history proved itself to be "right." Ultimately, force alone can
decide. And it is only through war that a nation or ideology dem-
onstrates its superiority over its competitors. "War is the creator
of all great things. All that is meaningful in the stream of life has
emerged through victory and defeat."

Hence for Spengler "the decisive problems lie, not in the
working-out of constitutions, but in the organization of a sound
working government." [7] It is not surprising, then, that he should
frequently express his admiration for the British system. Toward
England, Spengler shows a characteristically German combination of hostility and respect. The hostility, which comes out
strongly in *Prussianism and Socialism,* applies chiefly to what
Spengler regards as the catastrophic idea of importing English
political institutions into Germany. On the more abstract level,
Spengler can scarcely avoid citing England as a brilliant example
of his own theories. With their unwritten constitution and sure
sense for political realities, he finds, the British have done fàr
better than their continental neighbors who spent the whole nineteenth century in fruitless ideological debate and in tinkering with
their constitutional arrangements. Moreover, the British have
known how to retain the realities of aristocratic rule under the
forms of parliamentarism and democracy. Unfortunately, this

[6] *Decline,* II, 172, 368, 369, 441.
[7] *Ibid.,* II, 363, 368–369, 401.

happy compromise—along with the whole parliamentary phenomenon—is about to disappear before the onrush of the armed
Caesars.

From what we already know of Spengler's estimate of his
own century, it is not hard to deduce his attitude toward the
major political manifestations of his time. Most of them—electoral reform, democracy, the "working class"—he dismisses as
deceptive slogans serving to mask the true political power: finance
capital and its agent, the press. Quite naturally, he cares neither
for the slogans nor for what is behind them. But since he knows
that their reign will soon be over, he can regard the future with a
tempered optimism. Herewith begins that "positive" side of his
writing that his readers habitually neglected. Spengler rejoices
that there is awakening a "deep yearning for all old and worthy
tradition," that the "powers of the blood" are resuming their
"ancient lordship." But the time of the Caesars is still some decades away. Meantime the best policy for conservatives is to avoid
both of the "two most deadly kinds of idealism, the reactionary
and the democratic." They must learn to play the game of political parties—in which only their opponents now feel at home.
Against the day when great actions will again become possible,
they must cultivate all that remains sound in their ancient institutions:

> Every remnant of them, however tiny, that has kept itself
> alive in the being of any self-contained minority whatever
> will before long rise to incalculable values and bring about
> historical effects which no one yet imagines to be possible.
> The traditions of an old monarchy, of an old aristocracy, of
> an old polite society, in so much as they are still healthy
> enough to keep clear of professional or professorial politics,
> in so far as they possess honour, abnegation, discipline, the
> genuine sense of a great mission, . . . of duty and sacrifice—
> can become a centre which holds together the being-stream
> of an entire people and enables it to outlast this time and
> make its landfall in the future. To be "in condition" is every-

thing. It falls to us to live in the most trying times known to the history of a great Culture. The last race to keep its form, the last living tradition, the last leaders who have both at their back, will pass through and onward, victors.[8]

At this point Spengler leaves us in doubt as to whether the "last race" will be his own. But elsewhere in the *Decline,* he specifically names Germany as the "last nation of the West," and in the preface to his revised first volume he declares that he is "proud" to call his work a *"German philosophy."* [9] Such a profession of conventional national loyalty comes as something of a surprise from a writer with pretensions to detachment who envisages the future in terms of a supra-national uniformity presided over by Caesars and their personal followings. As we shall see when we come to analyze Spengler's racial theories, his view of these followings and of race in general conflicts sharply with that of nearly all other German nationalists. For him, Caesarism means the rule of an élite drawn without discrimination from all nationalities. How, then, can we account for his outbursts of Germanic pride? Partly, of course, we may detect a conscientious belief on Spengler's part that his nation, more than any other, regularly supplied the Faustian culture with its leading personalities; the *Decline* is heavily weighted with German examples. Yet this does not completely explain the inconsistency. We can only conclude that Spengler's national loyalty frequently got the better of his own theories, and that he permitted himself the luxury of hoping that it would be individual Germans, at the very least, who would play the leading role in the Caesarist era, and that a German, with a primarily German following, would finally emerge as the lord of all the minor Caesars.

Indeed, the chief importance of the political works is to reveal Spengler as far less sceptical, far more committed, than the original enunciation of his historical principles would have led us to expect. Aside from the chapter on the state, all of them are messages addressed to the German people—pleas to his coun-

[8] *Ibid.,* II, 430–432, 443, 464.   [9] *Ibid.,* I, xiv; II, 109.

trymen to grasp their historical opportunity to lead the Faustian imperium. Through sloth and misgovernment, Spengler feared, the Germans might fail to carry out the mission that was theirs by right of personal endowment. It was a very real sense of urgency, then, that led him to interrupt the composition of the second volume of the *Decline* to write his first political tract.

*   *   *

The original conception of *Prussianism and Socialism,* Albers tells us, came out of a long talk he had with Spengler in March of 1919. A few days before, with the assassination of Kurt Eisner, the short-lived Bavarian socialist republic had collapsed. It was natural that Albers should ask his learned friend what he thought of socialism in general. The reply was so striking that Albers suggested it be written up in book form. The following December *Prussianism and Socialism* appeared.[10]

As its starting point, Spengler's little volume took the German revolution of 1918 and, more particularly, the general disillusionment that had followed it. Although socialists of one sort or another had played the chief part in the revolution, a socialist state had not been established. As Spengler was writing, the National Assembly at Weimar was in the process of drawing up a constitution providing for a parliamentary republic not unlike the governments of Britain and France. This was what neither of the two major political forces in Germany had desired—neither the conservatives nor the representatives of the laboring masses. What had gone wrong?

The fault, Spengler found, lay in a tragic misunderstanding. The German socialists and the German conservatives thought themselves bitter enemies. In reality, they were in basic agreement. Their mutual hostility had permitted the real opponents of both of them—the advocates of parliamentary democracy—to win the constitutional battle. But this defeat need be only temporary. If the conservatives and socialists could come to realize their

[10] Albers, *op. cit.,* p. 129; "Preussentum und Sozialismus" is included in *Politische Schriften,* pp. 1–105.

fundamental similarity of aim, then they could unite to overthrow the Weimar settlement and establish a truly German form of government. The purpose of *Prussianism and Socialism*—as the title implied—was to prove the practicability of such an alliance.

The argument starts with one of the basic postulates of the *Decline*. As each culture has its unique "soul," so every nation or people within that culture has its own special interpretation of the more general spirit. To develop this national way of life, to unfold the potentialities of a given cultural bent, is the historical mission of each people. And every effort to organize a government or society in opposition to the national spirit will quite naturally yield unsatisfactory results.

From the springtime of the Faustian culture, Spengler finds, three European nations inherited universal ideals. The Spanish developed the idea of militant Catholicism. The English conquered primitive races in the name of a predatory, commercial notion of imperialism handed down to them by their Viking ancestors. The Prussians invented the bureaucratic service state. As opposed to these three masterful peoples, the French and Italians could conceive only limited political and cultural aims.

Such universal achievements Spengler calls "socialism"—in the sense of an ideal capable of dominating the entire world. But he also uses the term in a narrower sense, as a concept of cooperative enterprise under the guidance of a powerful, benevolent state. In this latter sense, the only people capable of being true socialists are the Prussians—or, more exactly, those Germans who have understood and absorbed into themselves the Prussian way of life. Hence any effort to establish parliamentary democracy in Germany is a kind of treason. It means imposing on the Germans a political ideal that has succeeded in England, because it has expressed the ruthless individualism of the English national spirit, but which for that very reason is out of place in Germany. Here constitutional, parliamentary democracy works as a "poison," and its advocates represent an "inner England," an alien element in German political life. "Of all the peoples of Western Europe," Spengler writes, "these two alone are marked by a strict social articulation." The one has an ethic of success, the other an ethic of duty. *"English society is founded on the distinction between rich and poor, Prussian society on the distinction between command and obedience. . . . Democracy in England means the possibility for everyone to become rich, in Prussia the possibility of attaining to every existing rank."* [11]

To find the basis of a correctly-organized German society we must go back to Frederick William I, the father of Frederick the Great and the founder of the Prussian tradition of military and bureaucratic discipline, to whom Spengler gives the paradoxical title of the "first conscious socialist." In the same tradition is Frederick the Great's familiar maxim: "I am the first servant of my state." [12] Bismarck too was following this principle of hierarchy and discipline when he founded the German Empire on military might. Seen in the perspective of "Prussian socialism," Bismarck's subsequent policy of social legislation was not a contradiction but rather a logical complement to the conservative tradition. And, in a different way, the founders of the great industrial cartels also made an essential contribution. Even August Bebel, the pre-war leader of German Social Democracy, was acting in the great tradition when he organized the German working class as a steadfast, disciplined fighting force.

If Bebel was a great German socialist, it was in spite of his ideological dependence on Marx. For Marx never understood the true principle of German socialism; he could never have appreciated the dictum "Every real German is a worker." The author of *Capital,* who lived the whole latter part of his life in England, founded his work on English conditions and developed his concept of socialism in an English context. His doctrine grew out of a typically British envy of the poor for the rich—coupled with Old Testament memories of an original curse on manual labor. The ideal of a Marxist-trained proletarian is to displace the capitalists—"expropriate the expropriators"—and like them to live a life of pleasant leisure. It is a private, a selfish, actually an unsocialist ideal. "Marxism is the capitalism of the working class."

[11] *Ibid.,* p. 45.   [12] *Ibid.,* pp. 38, 43.

True socialism—German socialism—"does not mean nationalization through expropriation or robbery."

In general, it is a question not of nominal possession but of the technique of administration. For a slogan's sake to buy up enterprises immoderately and purposelessly and to turn them over to public administration in place of the initiative and responsibility of their owners, who must eventually lose all power of supervision—that means the destruction of socialism. The old Prussian idea was to bring under legislative control the *formal* structure of the whole national productive force, at the same time carefully preserving the right of property and inheritance, and leaving scope for the kind of personal enterprise, talent, energy, and intellect displayed by an experienced chess player, playing within the rules of the game and enjoying *that sort* of freedom which the very sway of the rules affords. . . . Socialization means the slow transformation—taking centuries to complete—of the worker into an economic functionary, and the employer into a responsible supervisory official. . . .[13]

For a society conceived in these terms, corporatism is the logical form of government. Spengler states his requirements in unusually specific terms: "local corporate bodies organized according to the importance of each occupation to the people as a whole; higher representation in stages up to a supreme council of state; mandates revocable at any time; no organized parties, no professional politicians, no periodic elections." Over this "socialist" state, only a hereditary monarch can properly preside. But at the same time the state must be democratic. "Democracy, whatever one may think of it, is the political form of this century, which cannot fail to assert itself with success. There is no alternative . . . except democratization." This the conservatives must realize before it is too late. They must unite with the workers to fuse the ideals of Prussianism and socialism. Neither can be saved without the other.[14]

[13] *Ibid.*, pp. 10, 78, 80, 95.   [14] *Ibid.*, pp. 64, 69, 104.

And so we come to the final question: what sort of Caesarism will control the future? Who will rule the world imperium—the Germans or the English? There are no other candidates—except, perhaps, the Americans, who may be included with the British as heirs of the Anglo-Saxon tradition. Will it be a rule of "millionaires or generals, bankers or large-minded officials?" Will it be a "dictatorship of money or of organization, the world as booty or as a state, wealth or authority, success or vocation? . . . For it is the destiny of the world that is at stake." The conflict is unavoidable. It will be the decisive struggle of our civilization—as the struggle between Athens and Sparta was for the ancient world. These "*ideas* cannot be reconciled; the Viking spirit and the spirit of military order will fight it out to the finish, even though the world may emerge weary and broken from the blood bath of this century." [15]

*   *   *

When *Prussianism and Socialism* appeared, the public "rushed for it," full of excitement to learn what the author of the *Decline* had to say on so contemporary a topic. "The disappointment was universal. People began to whisper to each other that Spengler was nothing much, that he was a journalist, a reactionary, a phrase-maker, a pedant, a visionary. His mysterious fame quite clearly began to lose its aura of inviolability." [16] The publication of his first political tract had not a little to do with the sudden collapse of the Spengler vogue. Even as a political document, it had missed its mark. Spengler's ideas were too eccentric, they cut across too many party lines, to win any large number of adherents. Its author was palpably exaggerating when, thirteen years later, he claimed that *Prussianism and Socialism* had been the "point of departure" for the "national movement." [17]

Discouraged, perhaps, by this rebuff, and also because he was working hard on the second volume of the *Decline* and the

[15] *Ibid.*, pp. 53–55, 69, 71.
[16] Schroeter, *op. cit.*, quoting W. Wolfradt, p. 7*n*.
[17] Preface to *Politische Schriften*, p. vii.

revision of the first, Spengler made few public pronouncements during the four years following the publication of *Prussianism and Socialism*. Aside from the explanatory article "Pessimism?" and a lecture on the international position of Russia dating from 1922, we find practically nothing in his collected minor works until we reach the year 1924. Then suddenly we discover a burst of activity: in that year Spengler produced not only the second of his political tracts, *Reconstruction of the German Reich,* but also at least five political lectures in addition to the lecture on Nietzsche that has proved so helpful in determining the intellectual origins of the *Decline.*

Of course it may be that Spengler gave other lectures of which no record remains. We know that during the whole period of the 1920's he received frequent requests for articles and speeches. The preservation of some of them was purely accidental: Spengler kept no organized files, he destroyed his manuscripts, and he paid no attention to his miscellaneous lectures once they had served the purpose for which they had originally been composed.[18] On the other hand, the number of writings dating from 1924 seems more than accidental. It was the logical year for Spengler to make a major effort to arouse his countrymen. The previous year had seen the climax of Germany's post-war ordeal: in January, the French had occupied the Ruhr; in October, the Communists had taken up arms in Hamburg; in November, Hitler's beer-hall putsch had collapsed in ignominious failure; and in that same month, the national currency, after a summer and autumn of wild inflation, had at length been stabilized at the rate of a trillion old marks to one of the new. In 1923, Germany had hit the bottom: in 1924, she was already on solid ground. Not only the currency but all aspects of political and social life were rapidly stabilizing themselves. The time was now or never. It was Spengler's last chance to change his country's course before she should finally settle into the well-marked furrow of bourgeois constitutionalism.

Of the five political lectures dating from 1924 of which

[18] Editor's preface to *Reden und Aufsätze,* p. v.

copies have been preserved, two were largely incorporated in *Reconstruction of the German Reich*. One of them had been delivered to the Hamburg "Overseas Club" (in general, the sponsors of Spengler's lectures seem to have been the more prosperous element in society). A third was rather historical than polemical in tone. These three need not detain us. But a fourth—actually the first in date of delivery—is highly significant in that it represents the most dramatic and specific effort Spengler ever made to bring his ideas to bear on the German public—in this case, on the most pliable and impressionable segment of German society. The title is characteristic: "Political Duties of German Youth."

The occasion was a youth meeting in Würzburg in northern Bavaria held under the auspices of the Hochschulring Deutscher Art, a student movement deeply influenced by Spengler's political ideas. On that very day, February 26, Hitler's trial for high treason had opened in Munich. The atmosphere prickled with political passion. Spengler well knew that many of his young listeners sympathized openly or in secret with the tragi-comic hero of the beer-hall putsch. What he was going to say could scarcely be popular, and he later complained that the youth of Germany had not understood his message.[19]

For the lecture was the opening signal of that conflict between Spengler and National Socialism that will occupy us in the next chapter. The two could not avoid collision. If the "national movement" that Spengler had called for in *Prussianism and Socialism* had indeed materialized, it had turned out to be quite different from what he had originally intended. Hence Spengler's message to his young countrymen necessarily combined praise and blame in uneasy alternation. While congratulating them on their resolute hostility to the Versailles and Weimar settlements, he pleaded for a greater measure of political realism. He urged them not to serve the interests of Germany's enemies by noisily advertising their dissatisfaction with the terms of peace: surely their experience as soldiers or as duelists had taught them the

---

[19] Preface to *Politische Schriften*, p. x; "Politische Pflichten der deutschen Jugend" is included in this volume, pp. 127–156.

need of taking their adversaries by surprise. It was only by throwing away party programs and devoting themselves to the serious study of politics that the youth of Germany could perform their historical duty—to set for the twentieth century the sort of political model with which the ideas of the French Revolution and the practice of British parliamentarism had endowed the century preceding.

Unfavorable though the initial reaction may have been, this lecture aroused widespread discussion among German youth groups.[20] Three months later, Spengler's *Reconstruction of the German Reich* was published. If *Prussianism and Socialism* represented a fall from the level of the *Decline,* Spengler's second political tract dropped a stage lower still. It was neither well-phrased nor well-organized. Rather than presenting a consecutive argument, it offered a series of miscellaneous suggestions for the guidance of "future statesmen." [21] The several essays that Spengler had strung together to make up his little book varied greatly in style and emphasis. The first was an intemperate and vulgar attack on the whole Weimar dispensation; the erstwhile Olympian author of the *Decline* stooped to report the most irresponsible gossip—even to the point of accusing the leaders of German Social Democracy of getting drunk "with naked dancing girls . . . while delegations of workers waited at the gate." [22] The other chapters were more practical, and at least hold some interest today as indications of Spengler's point of view on a variety of controversial topics: we learn that he condemned the income and inheritance taxes as "fiscal Bolshevism;" that he advised the creation of an aristocracy of labor to break the hold of Marxist-minded trade unions on the German working classes; that he advocated a liberalization of the traditional system of admission and promotion in the German bureaucracy; and that he hoped for a reform of education in which a greater emphasis on practical

[20] Else Frobenius, *Mit uns zieht die neue Zeit: Eine Geschichte der deutschen Jugendbewegung* (Berlin, 1927), pp. 250–251.

[21] Preface to *Politische Schriften,* p. xi; "Neubau des Deutschen Reiches" is included in this volume, pp. 185–296.

[22] *Ibid.,* p. 194.

subjects, sport, and general reading would culminate in the foundation of élite schools on the model of Eton. All this, however,
added up to very little. In *Reconstruction of the German Reich,*
the stream of Spengler's creative thinking was running exceedingly thin.

In the same month of May in which this volume appeared,
Spengler delivered the fifth of his political lectures. From a social
standpoint this address marked the high-point of his career. As
Spengler had lectured the youth of his country on their "duties,"
now he was to talk to the German nobility about their "tasks."
For the son of an obscure postal official, for a political writer
with a deeply-rooted feeling for birth and hierarchy, it must have
been exceedingly gratifying to be asked to address the annual
assembly of the German aristocracy, which in that year was held
in Breslau. At last Spengler had an opportunity to put his ideas
before the segment of society he respected the most.

His message could scarcely have come as a surprise to those
of his aristocratic hearers who had read the *Decline.* The very
fact that he had been invited to speak indicated that the nobles
knew very well he would have nothing displeasing to say. A strong
nobility, Spengler told them, was alone fitted to maintain a
nation's political tradition. Such a tradition, as the example of
England had proved, could compensate for an absence of out-
standing statesmen for decades at a stretch. It was dangerous for
Germany simply to await the chance arrival of another Bismarck.
Meantime she required an élite of disinterested patriots to uphold
her political tradition at a high level. "Particularly in Germany,"
Spengler reasoned, where there existed "no middle-class society
of distinction" as in England and France, the maintenance of a
nobility "as the center of its leading classes" was clearly indispensable.[23]

*   *   *

We know of no reaction to this address either on the part of
the nobles themselves or from the general public. By the time

---

[23] "Aufgaben des Adels" is included in *Reden und Aufsätze,* pp. 89–95.

Spengler delivered it he must have realized that his great effort had been in vain—that all this exhorting and appealing had beaten against closed minds. Still less successful than his first campaign of 1919, this second effort of 1924 had failed to move his countrymen. As he had felt his admirers slipping away from him, his tone had grown more arrogant, more querulous—but all to no avail. For the next five years, Germany was to enjoy its sole period of relative stability. Happy to rest from their worries and to participate in the general prosperity, people no longer interested themselves in theories of cultural doom or in elaborate projects for a corporative reorganization of the state. Even conservatives and monarchists, under the leadership of old Field Marshal von Hindenburg—since 1925 president of the Reich—began to give grudging support to the republican regime. And the educated world had found a new philosopher in the austere existentialist Heidegger.

Yet the political ideas that Spengler had offered would appear at first sight to have been just about what a majority of Germans wanted. A maintenance of the traditional hierarchies, but democratized and thrown open to new talent, the preservation of private enterprise, but subject to the ultimate control of the state—the formula was appealing in its very contradictions. From the Romantics to present-day Christian Democracy, such ideas, in a variety of incarnations, have haunted the minds of Germans dissatisfied with the sharper alternatives offered by traditional absolutism and the more usual forms of parliamentary government. This sort of corporatism seemed to constitute a truly *German* solution, as opposed to the "superficial" legalisms of the British and the French. Yet Spengler and the other neo-conservatives of the early twenties had succeeded in imposing their ideas neither on the parties nor on the public. Why had they failed?

In its very reconciliation of opposites lay the weakness of Spengler's appeal. Its artfully-devised compromises really satisfied nobody. None of the organized pressure groups in society wanted exactly what Spengler had proposed. To traditional monarchists, his ideas seemed dangerously eccentric and visionary.

The great industrialists desired freedom from state control—or at least protection by a regime that could be counted on to serve their interests. The organized workers naturally distrusted a writer who took no pains to conceal his dislike of trade-unionism and Social Democracy and his admiration for the upper classes. For white-collar people ruined by the inflation—who might have been expected to be Spengler's most eager listeners—his ideas were not nearly radical enough. The author of the *Decline* might claim to be making proposals for the "civilization" phase of Western history—democratic by very necessity. But he was constantly betraying a nostalgia for the forms of an aristocratic society left over from an era that he himself had consigned to the irrevocably-vanished past.

For all the truly dissatisfied, there awaited an unsavory collection of demagogues—Hitler among them—who could outbid Spengler any day in the glitter and violence of their appeal. No mere scholar, no matter how unconventional, could hope to compete with a band of ruffians like these. Nor could he compete with the constituted powers, the party leaders of the Weimar settlement, who were able to offer what the average citizen understandably longed for after five years of continuous turmoil—social peace and financial security. The Republic might be unexciting, but it at least guaranteed an honest and fairly efficient administration. Nationalist demagoguery and parliamentary government were solid facts: against them Spengler could oppose only the imaginative power of his historical vision—and this was wearing thin. Perhaps Spengler had been untrue to his own best knowledge in ever embarking on the career of a political polemicist. In the second volume of the *Decline,* he had insisted on the irrelevance of ideological writing and the futility of political theory.[24]

And so Spengler had fallen between two stools in trying to be both a conservative and a prophet of political reform. Nor was this the end of his inconsistencies. In the attempt to write both popular propaganda and scholarly theory, he had failed to do either of them very well. If Spengler was an ineffective political

[24] *Decline,* II, 17–18.

agitator, he was an equally poor theoretician. Much of what he wrote about politics was quite penetrating. But it had all been said—and infinitely better—by someone else. His critique of electoral democracy and Marxism, with its concomitant rejection of all ideologies, was the common coin of twentieth-century political theory. And so far as Marxism was concerned, he was unable to come to grips with its economic doctrines in the fashion of a trained economist like Pareto; Spengler's knowledge of economics was perhaps the weakest link in his academic preparation. The center of Spengler's theory—the notion of élites and the necessary rule of a social class—was simply second-rate Pareto. In the four years immediately preceding the publication of *Prussianism and Socialism,* the great Italian theorist had put the same ideas in far more sophisticated language in his *Treatise of General Sociology.* Spengler's sole remotely original contribution had been the paradoxical union of the concepts of Prussian nationalism and socialism. And this unholy marriage—which stretched the second term beyond all theoretical recognition—was to have a violent and bloody history from whose early aberrations even Spengler recoiled in disgust.

In his political phase, then, the author of the *Decline* could only diminish the reputation he had won by his earlier work. For us today his political writings are of no wider interest than as additions to our knowledge of their author's own mentality and of the times in which he lived. As political propagandist, Spengler is a symptom rather than a creator.

* * *

The years from 1924 to 1927 were less agitated than the preceding half-decade of Spengler's life. Although he continued to write articles and deliver lectures and was constantly at work on his "metaphysical" project, he produced no finished writing during these years. Now that it had again become financially possible for Germans to travel, Spengler was frequently abroad. Two at least of these journeys had a political motive. In 1923, he had visited the exiled German Crown Prince in Holland, and in 1924, during a lecture tour to Sweden, Finland, and the Baltic states, he was asked by the Foreign Office to take confidential soundings of Russian influence in that area. For the Soviet Union itself, however, he was unable to obtain an entry visa. A year later, Spengler resumed his pre-war practice of making frequent trips to Italy— particularly to Rome, the Italian city that quite naturally interested him most.

Gradually, too, Spengler had begun to make acquaintanceships and to win a modest following in the German academic world. Through Leo Frobenius (of whom more later) he had at length come into contact with a circle of like-minded scholars. And in 1927, there began to appear the first substantial historical work that clearly showed his influence. In the introduction to his brilliant and erratic history of European culture, Egon Friedell referred to Spengler as "perhaps the most powerful and vivid thinker to appear on German soil since Nietzsche" and spoke of himself as "in the enviable position of being able to make use of Spengler." [25]

From 1927 on, ill health seriously interfered with Spengler's writing. The headaches that had originally driven him from Hamburg, and about which he had frequently complained to Albers at the time he was working on the second volume of the *Decline,* had evidently grown much more severe. In 1927, he suffered a slight stroke, and during the next three years he could do very little work. At least he was less lonely than in the past. Two years earlier, his sister Hildegard had come to live with him, bringing with her her daughter, also called Hildegard, who was to serve as his literary executor after his death. With them, Spengler convalesced from his stroke in Switzerland, and in the following year he was strong enough to make a more extended journey to Southern France and Spain.

Under the surface of this physical suffering, we also catch from time to time the reflection of a deeper mental anguish.

---

[25] Egon Friedell, *Kulturgeschichte der Neuzeit,* I (Munich, 1927); translated by Charles Francis Atkinson as *A Cultural History of the Modern Age,* I (New York, 1930), pp. 37, 41.

Spengler never wrote about his own feelings. His personal code of proud stoicism and iron self-mastery dictated silence on everything that touched him really closely. But in his posthumously-published *Thoughts*, we can find here and there an aphorism that seems to have grown out of hard personal experience. "A true man," Spengler wrote, "wants to have children." But a "higher type of man, a creator of meaningful works, has no inner need of children, and therefore, for men of real genius, marriage—but not sexual love—is illogical." The man of genius, Spengler noted elsewhere, "lives in such a way that his existence becomes a sacrifice to his idea." [26] This was the course that Spengler had chosen. With open eyes he had decided for personal loneliness and dedication to what he believed to be his mission. Only this once did he betray what the choice had cost him.

And beyond the question of personal sacrifice, there was a further torment. Spengler was trying to be two things at once. He was both a man of books, living the withdrawn life of a devoted scholar, and a would-be man of action, scorning the pedantries of the learned world. To his American publisher, he more than once expressed a "playful desire" to throw all his books into the river.[27] The two tendencies were quite literally tearing Spengler apart. Occasionally, as in his earliest literary exercise, he might attempt to bring them together on a level of high abstraction. He was doubtless thinking also of himself when he said of Nietzsche: "Because all action was so alien to him and he only knew how to think, for that very reason he understood better than any great man of deeds, the wellsprings of human action." [28] It might be consoling to reflect that one was that rare type of individual who, knowing better than the men of action themselves what their deeds really meant, was uniquely equipped to be their counsellor. But of what use was such a talent when the doers of this world had refused to listen?

[26] *Gedanken*, pp. 4, 122.
[27] Recollections of Alfred A. Knopf, in Dakin, *op. cit.*, biographical note, p. 359.
[28] "Nietzsche und sein Jahrhundert," *Reden und Aufsätze*, p. 122.

CHAPTER EIGHT

SPENGLER AND
NATIONAL SOCIALISM

AT the turn of the new decade, Spengler roused himself for a major effort. Perhaps suspecting that he would never live to complete his "metaphysical" project, he published a fragment of it in the form of a long essay. Meanwhile he had embarked on another study—a history of the pre-civilization stage of human development—which had gradually fused with the earlier undertaking. Thus the little book entitled *Man and Technics* that Spengler published in 1931 represented gleanings from both these projects: it was first—as its subtitle stated—"a contribution to a philosophy of life;" but it was also a kind of anthropological fantasy. In its violent style and unashamedly fragmentary sequences of thought, it reflected the difficult circumstances of its composition. Of all Spengler's works, it is the hardest to classify and, as an intellectual construction, the least successful.

The last chapter of the *Decline* Spengler had entitled "The Machine." The theme of an unceasing struggle between nature and humanity that this chapter had merely sketched out, *Man and Technics* developed into an explicit theory. Its outlines were not particularly novel. Aside from one or two specifically Spenglerian touches—such as the characterization of man as a beast of prey, *"the highest form of mobile life"*—the earlier part of the book was simply a schematic and rather fanciful account of the origin of tribal life and settled communities. But with the advent of a

120

technological society, the argument began to gather momentum. "Every work of man," Spengler announced, "is artificial, unnatural. . . . This is the beginning of man's *tragedy*—for Nature is the stronger of the two." Witness the ruin of all past civilizations. "The fight against Nature is hopeless and yet—it will be fought out to the bitter end." [1]

In this artificial character of technics Spengler discovers what Toynbee was later to call the "nemesis" of civilization— more particularly of our Faustian society, which has pushed technology to its most daring limits. At the present time, Spengler asserts, such a nemesis is rapidly overtaking us. The "group of nations of Nordic blood under the leadership of British, Germans, French, and Americans" that up to now has dominated the world through its technical proficiency and near monopoly of exploitable coal resources, is obviously losing its grip. This process manifests itself in four ways. First, technology is outrunning its usefulness: we multiply machines without regard to whether they actually improve our lives; from their masters, we are becoming their servants. Second, the hands who run the machines are in revolt against the caste of technical directors; they no longer appreciate the latters' unique contribution and argue that they can easily be dispensed with. Third, these technical leaders themselves are failing: the level of scientific education, which ought to be constantly on the rise, threatens to become stationary. And the "strong and creative talents . . . are turning away from practical problems and sciences and towards pure speculation. . . . *The flight of the born leader from the Machine is beginning.*" [2] Finally, the "colored" races—the black and yellow peoples to whom the Faustian world has most recklessly imparted its technical knowledge—will soon turn these arts against their inventors. Already they can undersell the products of Western industry. Eventually they will conquer the Western nations themselves.

[1] Oswald Spengler, *Der Mensch und die Technik: Beitrag zu einer Philosophie des Lebens* (Munich, 1931); translated by Charles Francis Atkinson as *Man and Technics: A Contribution to a Philosophy of Life* (New York, 1932), pp. 22, 44–45.

[2] *Ibid.*, pp. 90–97.

This conquest will mark the end of technology as we know it today. To the "colored," technical progress is not—as to the Westerner—a necessity of life; "it is but a weapon in their fight against the Faustian civilization." The struggle, for us, is ultimately hopeless. Nevertheless, "our duty is to hold on to the lost position, without hope, without rescue, like that Roman soldier whose bones were found in front of a door in Pompeii, who, during the eruption of Vesuvius, died at his post because they forgot to relieve him." [3]

Man and Technics hardly ruffled the surface of the educated world. It indicated only too clearly that Spengler had fallen behind and out of intellectual circulation, that his work could no longer bear up against the competition of more rigorously trained minds. As an amateur venture into anthropology, *Man and Technics* was merely embarrassing. The charitable reader might note an occasional new idea: he might detect a more pessimistic tone than in any of Spengler's other works. But even this was largely a question of emphasis. Depressed by illness and neglect, Spengler seems to have turned to speculating on what would follow the Faustian civilization, and to have abandoned, temporarily at least, the more cheerful pursuit of picking candidates for its imperial mantle. He appears to have fallen into doubt as to whether the Western world would have the time to organize such an imperium before it was overwhelmed by barbarians from without. The notion of a "colored" peril was anything but original. From its intellectually disreputable discoverers—chiefly Germans and Americans—it had passed fitfully through Spengler's earlier writings. But the prominence it assumed in *Man and Technics* was something new. It foreshadowed the central theme of Spengler's last political work—*The Hour of Decision*—the book that was to bring him into open conflict with the Nazis.

*   *   *

The year following the publication of *Man and Technics* witnessed Spengler's third and final effort to win over the German

[3] *Ibid.,* pp. 103–104.

public to his political program. Once again, the situation had become fluid; once again, the opportunity offered for an unorthodox intellectual to find a hearing. In the last months of the year 1929, with the death of the Republic's most eminent statesman, Gustav Stresemann, and the beginning of the world economic crisis, Germany's quiet period had abruptly come to an end. The next three years were to see the gradual dissolution of the republican regime. With unemployment steadily growing and a majority of the population a prey to severe economic hardship, the advocates of extreme solutions again began to attract adherents. The nationalist and racist demagogues, who during the previous five years had barely been able to keep their movements together, now saw new supporters flocking to their standards. Conservatives and nationalists began openly to desert the Republic to which they had so recently pledged a doubtful loyalty, and to contemplate alliance with the agitators of the streets. For two years, under the chancellorship of Heinrich Brüning, the government maintained a semblance of order and legality. But by 1932, the Republic was obviously *in extremis*. The succession alone was in doubt: would it go to the Communists, to the traditional conservatives, or to the fascist and racist movements that had finally united under the leadership of Adolf Hitler? Naturally, for Spengler, only the second of these choices was at all welcome. And his efforts to stiffen the hesitant conservatives by a strong reaffirmation of national principles could not fail eventually to bring down upon him the unforgiving wrath of the National Socialists.

Although Spengler might occasionally speak of a "Third Reich" as a *"Germanic ideal,"* the connotation these words carried for him was vague and unpolitical, an inheritance from medieval mysticism.[4] It had only a remote connection with the very specific projects of the Nazis. But this—like other Spenglerian phrases—has been responsible for a good deal of confusion concerning the precise relation between the author of the *Decline* and National Socialism. Outside Germany at least, he has generally been listed among Hitler's precursors. This reputation is not

[4] See, for example, *Decline*, I, 363.

totally undeserved. But it is applicable to Spengler only in a very special sense—and only after a host of modifications and extenuating circumstances have been advanced.

Spengler's earliest recorded references to National Socialism appear in that lecture of 1924 in which he scolded the youth of Germany for their lack of political realism. The Nazis and their competitors, he complained, had turned politics into a kind of "intoxication." They had inspired the nation's youth with enthusiasm for trifles—"colors and badges, music and processions, theatrical vows and amateurish appeals and theories." They seemed to forget that a successful policy had "never yet been made with the heart alone." Far wiser were the Italian Fascists, whose emphasis on "results" rather than on "programs and parades" had permitted them "to come to a well-timed understanding with the controlling economic powers." [5]

Later in the same year, in *Reconstruction of the German Reich,* Spengler turned his criticism against the Nazis' racial theories. Race-feelings, he argued, offered no sound basis for *Realpolitik.* History had proved that in accepting leaders of foreign origin—a Catherine the Great, a Napoleon, a Disraeli—Germany's competitors had profited by their lack of prejudice. Good Germans, he concluded, must remember "that the most dangerous anti-German traits, the inclination toward international and pacifist enthusiasm, the hatred for authority and acts of power, are deeply rooted in the *German* character itself. Members of one's own race are always more dangerous than strangers, who, for the very reason that they are a minority, must prefer assimilation, if they are seriously given the choice." [6]

It was this attitude toward race that most profoundly separated Spengler from the National Socialists. Already in the second volume of the *Decline* he had clearly outlined his own theories. For Spengler, as for Nietzsche, the idea of a "folk" was simply a vaporous creation of German Romanticism. True race

[5] "Politische Pflichten der deutschen Jugend," *Politische Schriften*, pp. 148, 153.

[6] "Neubau des Deutschen Reiches," *Politische Schriften*, pp. 202–203.

had nothing to do with the language people spoke. Nor was it a matter of blood, of biological inheritance; such notions belonged in the rubbish-heap along with the other relics of the Darwinian age. Race was nothing more than a product of geographical influences—and of common feelings arising out of a common history.

Hence race manifested itself not in bodily characteristics but in the sense of form and tradition exemplified by certain rare individuals. Far from being scientifically identifiable, it was an intangible essence, to be grasped only through "physiognomic" feeling. As a connoisseur can judge at a glance the qualities of a fine horse, so also "we all know a man of race, a 'thoroughbred,' when we see one. . . . In the last resort every individual man and every individual moment of his existence have their own race." [7] It would be the task of the new Caesars, then, to seek out men of race, without prejudice, wherever they might be found, and through the sharing of great deeds to fuse their followers into a new people.

In line with this highly personal theory, Spengler necessarily viewed the Jewish question in a radically different fashion from the Nazis. To Spengler, the Jews were a people formed by a very special history and tradition, who, like any other strongly-defined group, regularly produced their share of individuals "of race." But the Jews had represented an alien element among the peoples of Europe, and the latter had had good reason for hating them. To this extent, Spengler agreed with the anti-Semitic propagandists. Yet he found that the modern racists based their dislike on totally erroneous theories. It was not the difference between Semitic and "Aryan" speech or "blood" that was responsible for the hostility between Jews and Christians. It was rather a clash of cultural heritage. Throughout the Middle Ages, the Jews had lived in Europe as cultural fossils—relics of the decaying Magian civilization stranded in the youthful Faustian world. Jealously maintaining their own traditions, they never cared to understand the spiritual forces that moved their neighbors. To the Faustian concept of national loyalty, they opposed the old Magian ideal of

[7] *Decline*, II, 124, 131.

a supra-national consensus of the faithful. The wars, the dynastic ambitions of the European states quite understandably left them cold. It was not until the eighteenth century that Jews and Faustians began to understand each other. Then, with the new ideal of the Enlightenment, the Christian world itself began to build an international consensus of men of tolerance and universal sympathies. In this endeavor, the Jews could join with enthusiasm—although they actually appreciated the Enlightenment only in its negative and destructive aspects.

The Enlightenment—and its successor movements in the nineteenth and twentieth centuries—gradually broke down the barriers between Jew and Christian. In destroying the cultural traditions of both of them, it prepared the way for their eventual fusion. The present century would see the final dissolution of Christian and Jewish nationality alike in the common anonymity of a "civilized" society. For the modern Jew, the only possible course was complete assimilation.[8]

On the racial question, then, as on nearly every other subject, Spengler clung tenaciously to an eccentric position of his own. And, like his other theories, his racial doctrines offered a curious mixture of fantasy and good sense. His emphasis on geographical influence, his intuitive cult of the "thoroughbred" man, carried mystical overtones that constantly threatened to swell into an unorthodox racism of their own. In his passages on the Jews, his tone betrayed a disquieting mixture of antipathy and admiration. And toward the "colored" his later writings revealed a growing hostility. But against the grosser and more common forms of racism Spengler offered a stubborn resistance. He clearly saw through the superficiality of classifications by language, and the scientific impossibility of the doctrine of Aryan "blood." Thus to Spengler the theories closest to the Nazis' hearts were manifest absurdities. Naturally he was unwilling to combat them in the name of universal humanitarianism: he would not be so untrue to his own ideas as to fight one delusion with the slogans of what he believed to be another. But he was prepared to unleash the full

[8] *Ibid.*, II, 315–323.

force of his scorn and ridicule in an attempt to dissuade the German people from a course that he was sincerely convinced could lead only to a fruitless and dangerous dissipation of their energies.

*   *   *

Nineteen thirty-two, then, was to be the year of Spengler's last great effort. In the autumn of that year, Beck brought out a "popular edition" of Spengler's collected political works. The author's preface was a kind of retrospective manifesto. In it he repeated his condemnation of Hitler: what he had said in 1924 held true in 1932 *"with undiminished force;"* the leader of the national movement, he declared, in his most celebrated anti-Nazi quip, should be a "hero," not a "heroic tenor." Then, after affirming that he had composed his lectures and political tracts "not for the moment but for the future," Spengler concluded:

> I see more keenly than others because I do my thinking independently of parties, tendencies, and interests. . . . I feel lonelier than ever—not as though I were among the blind, but as though I were with people who have covered their eyes so as not to see the collapse of a house against which they are beating with little hammers. . . . When will people finally begin to hear and not merely read? I am waiting.[9]

During that same autumn, Spengler had been writing what was to be his last political work. It was an outgrowth and expansion of a lecture entitled "Germany in Danger" that he had delivered at Hamburg in 1929. Evidently the writing and printing went on virtually simultaneously, since we learn that it had been printed "up to page 106" by January 1933, when the Nazis came to power. This event faced Spengler with a serious dilemma. What he had written was sure to displease the new rulers of Germany, who might even go so far as to suppress the book entirely. Yet it was not in Spengler's nature to withdraw or alter anything that he had said. Eventually—and apparently with some

---

[9] Preface to *Politische Schriften,* pp. x, xiii.

reluctance—he decided to take at least a minimum of precautions. Without changing a word of his manuscript, he simply cut it off where it was—60-odd pages beyond what had already been printed—and published this fragment as a "first volume" under a new and less provocative title. During the summer, shortly before the book appeared, he added an introduction softening somewhat the severity of the text to follow.[10]

In this introduction Spengler announced that he would "neither scold nor flatter," that he would "refrain from forming any estimate of those things which are only just coming into being."

> So much, however, can be said already: the national revolution of 1933 was a mighty phenomenon and will remain such in the eyes of the future by reason of the elemental, super-personal force with which it came and the spiritual discipline with which it was carried through. Here was something Prussian through and through, . . . which transformed souls in one moment. . . . But all the more must those who took part realize that this was no victory, for opponents were lacking. . . . It was a promise of *future* victories that have yet to be won by hard fighting, and merely cleared the ground for these. The leaders bear the full responsibility therefor, and it is for them to know, or to learn, the significance of it all. The task is fraught with immense dangers, and its sphere lies not within the boundaries of Germany but beyond, in the realm of wars and catastrophes where world politics alone speak. Germany is, more than any other country, bound up with the fate of all the others.

Hence Spengler could only view "with misgiving" the way in which Hitler's triumph was being "noisily celebrated from day to day. It were better to save our enthusiasm for a day of real and definitive results. . . . And if no one else has the courage to see

[10] Introduction to *Hour of Decision*, p. xv; Hildegard Kornhardt, " 'Deutschland in Gefahr:' Fragmente zum II. Band der 'Jahre der Entscheidung'/ Von Oswald Spengler," *Echo der Woche* (Munich), September 17, 1948, p. 6.

and to tell what it is he sees, I mean to do so. I have a *right* to criticism since by means of it I have repeatedly demonstrated that which *must* happen because it will *happen.*" [11]

The book itself certainly contained several highly unflattering references to the Nazis. Spengler did not hesitate to call them "everlasting 'Youths' " and to accuse them of raving "like mendicant friars." [12] But these were side remarks and formed only a small part of the whole. On the strength of such statements alone, *The Hour of Decision* could scarcely figure as an anti-Nazi polemic.

The bulk of the book offered nothing more than a repetition of Spengler's earlier themes. We find the familiar attacks on Marxist-minded labor leaders and the more recent obsession with the "colored" peril, coupled with a reiteration of the doctrine of races as *"elective affinities."* [13] For the development of Spengler's thought, however, two things are significant—the discussion of Italian Fascism, in which Spengler for the first time attempted to assess the historical role of this new political phenomenon; and the statements on Germany's international situation, which expressed his final position on the Faustian imperium.

Fascism, Spengler declared, was simply a transition regime:

> What anticipates the future is not the being of Fascism as a party, but simply and solely the figure of its creator. Mussolini is no party leader . . .; he is the *lord* of his country. . . . Mussolini is first and foremost a statesman, ice-cold and sceptical, realist, diplomat. . . . Mussolini is a master-man with the Southern cunning of the race in him, like the condottieri of the Renaissance, and is therefore able to stage his movement in entire consonance with the character of Italy —home of opera—without ever being intoxicated by it himself. . . .

"As a mass party with noise and disturbance and . . . oratory," Italian Fascism had remained back in the era of political agita-

---

[11] *Hour of Decision,* pp. x–xii, xiv.
[12] *Ibid.,* pp., 13, 101.   [13] *Ibid.,* p. 58.

tion. But in the figure of Mussolini it had served the future by providing a model for the Caesars to come.[14]

In returning to the theme of Faustian world-leadership that he had temporarily abandoned in *Man and Technics,* Spengler revised and combined his earlier attitudes, to give his countrymen the clearest possible steer. His new conviction of the overriding importance of the "colored" peril—and he included Russia among the "colored" nations—led him to insist less strongly than before on the national hostilities within the Western world. The Faustians, Spengler urged, should drop their petty quarrels and unite to resist the barbarian menace from without. Hence *The Hour of Decision* did not repeat the prediction of an inevitable and final struggle between Germany and England with which *Prussianism and Socialism* had concluded. Without making any direct attacks on the British, Spengler confined himself to the assertion that the English nation was "neither . . . strong, young, or healthy enough, spiritually and racially, to combat this terrible crisis with confidence." [15] For other reasons, both France and the United States had disqualified themselves. There remained only Germany.

"Why is the German people," Spengler asked, "the least exhausted of the white world, and therefore the one on which may be placed the most hope? Because its political past has given it no opportunity to *waste* its precious blood and its great abilities. This is the one blessed aspect of our wretched history since 1500: it has used us *sparingly.*" Thwarted of a great history, Germany had preserved a certain "barbarism"—"strong race, the eternal warlike in the type of the beast-of-prey man." Against the new barbarians, it could serve as the shield of an old civilization by steadfastly gathering together all that remained of its primitive and traditional virtues.[16]

*　　*　　*

The Nazis did not react immediately. Although Hitler failed to acknowledge the complimentary copy that had been sent him,

[14] *Ibid.,* pp. 186–188.　　[15] *Ibid.,* p. 73.　　[16] *Ibid.,* p. 225.

twelve thousand other copies had already been sold before the authorities took alarm. And the original press attacks served only to promote further sales. It was three months after publication— and when 150 thousand copies were in print—that the government finally forbade the mention of Spengler's name in the press and took measures to stop the sale of his book. These measures achieved the desired effect—but they could not prevent the surreptitious circulation of the thousands of copies that were already in the hands of the public.[17]

Among the chorus of Nazi voices that joined in condemning *The Hour of Decision,* at least one spoke officially for the party. In a widely-circulated pamphlet, Johann von Leers, Leader of the Division of Foreign Policy and Foreign Information in the German High School for Politics, sought to disabuse the German public of the impression—apparently fairly common—that Spengler's philosophy was good Nazism. Far from being anything of the kind, Leers argued, *The Hour of Decision* was a counter-revolutionary tract. Its author was a merely negative sceptic, an enemy of the workers, with an "ice-cold contempt for the people," whose real desire was to return to the "old aristocratic society" of the eighteenth century.[18] Spengler understood neither race nor the "folk" idea. And his chief racial doctrine—the "colored" menace—was a dangerous error, since it taught Germany to distrust Japan, her natural ally, to the neglect of her real enemies in Europe.

Other critics warned against the fragmentary and oblique character of Spengler's writing, which left his less sophisticated readers in doubt as to what he actually meant. Moreover, they belittled his anti-Nazi statements as a kind of family treachery. "Hypnotized by his own intellectual construction and blinded by prejudice," Spengler had failed to recognize "his own children." [19] This was the real reason for the Nazis' rage. They had always

[17] Kornhardt, " 'Deutschland in Gefahr,' " p. 6.

[18] Johann v. Leers, *Spenglers weltpolitisches System und der Nationalsozialismus* (Berlin, 1934), pp. 6–7, 25.

[19] Arthur Zweiniger, *Spengler im Dritten Reich: Eine Antwort auf Oswald Spenglers "Jahre der Entscheidung"* (Oldenburg i. O., 1933), p. 12.

regarded Spengler as one of theirs—unorthodox, perhaps, and frequently unkind, but a true precursor of the "national revolution." Now, at the very moment when he might have been expected to discard his former reservations, he had definitively turned away from them. It had taken a while for this conviction to penetrate the rather slow-moving National Socialist mind. The offending book itself did not immediately reveal its unacceptable character: as we have seen, the anti-Nazi passages were a minor element in a basically nationalist argument that did not differ too much from what Hitler himself was saying. But when they had finally understood what Spengler was driving at, the Nazis turned on him with all the fury of disappointed expectation. For Spengler had done two unforgivable things: he had clearly repudiated the National Socialists as the wrong people to lead the revolution for which he, like them, had been working for fifteen years; and he had openly advocated the things that Hitler was going to do but did not care to have advertised before the outside world— the preservation of Germany's traditional ruling classes and the attainment of world hegemony through war. It was this personal independence and over-frankness about goals which he held in common with them that drove the Nazis to bitter recrimination. Compared to these sins, the question of a merely intellectual heresy on such a matter as race was distinctly secondary.

In thus condemning Spengler as a precursor gone wrong, the Nazis showed a surer sense of his historical position than did the author of the *Decline* himself in posing as their enemy. For, in an objective sense, Spengler *had* served as their precursor. In undermining public confidence in the Republic and in parliamentary institutions, and in preaching the association of the concepts of Prussianism and socialism, he had prepared the way for the Nazi mentality. In blurring all ideological lines, in rejecting ideology itself as a sentimental illusion, he had aided in that process of intellectual softening-up by which Hitler was eventually to profit. Spengler had played with fire. He had tossed off wild phrases about a "hard" philosophy of life, about blood and destruction, that could not fail to be misunderstood. Personally, he might advocate the rule of a cultivated aristocracy. But once he had helped to launch the forces of violence, he was powerless to keep them within the bounds of "form" and "style." The plea that Spengler differed radically from the Nazis on many specific points and that he rejected their leadership of the national revolution has more intellectual than historical validity. When Hitler had come to power, it was courageous of Spengler to protest that this was not what he had desired. But it could not alter the responsibility of the author of the *Decline* along with that of many another European intellectual who recoiled—too late—from what his words had helped to bring to pass.

*   *   *

The Nazi condemnation of *The Hour of Decision* was actually a blessing in disguise. In forcing Spengler to abandon political writing, it drove him back to his earlier and—for us today—more permanently significant interests. During the last three years of his life, the author of the *Decline,* although personally unmolested, lived under a nearly complete official boycott. An occasional writer might still hail him as a precursor of National Socialism, along with such other unorthodox prophets as Wagner, Nietzsche, Moeller van den Bruck, and Stefan George.[20] But for the official propagandists of the regime, the watchword was total silence.

Under these circumstances, it was out of the question for Spengler to publish any more of *The Hour of Decision.* The second volume would have to wait until "after the deluge." From time to time, Spengler added to his notes—bitter, frequently sarcastic comments on the events of the day. Taken as a whole, they are of little interest and show no change in Spengler's thinking. Only occasionally do we find a flash of prophetic understanding —as in the prediction of a "march on Moscow" that would end "as with Napoleon." These occasional notes were apparently the sole vestige of his former political activity. Otherwise he had

[20] See, for example, Herbert Schack, *Denker und Deuter: Männer vor der deutschen Wende* (Stuttgart, 1938), pp. 107–125.

come to the sensible decision to devote himself "to the second millennium before Christ," since he was not permitted to write about the second millennium of his own era.[21]

The work to which Spengler was referring was the old "metaphysical" project. Now at last he was compelled by sheer necessity to give it his full attention. This project—as we have seen at the beginning of the chapter—had fairly early in Spengler's literary career merged with another undertaking, a history of primitive humanity. The latter was an outgrowth of one of Spengler's rare intellectual acquaintanceships. In 1920, at the time when he was working on the second volume of the *Decline,* he had come into contact with the African specialist Leo Frobenius and his circle of philosophical anthropologists. Inspired by the writings of the historian Johann Jakob Bachofen—like Burckhardt and Nietzsche, a professor at Basel—this group had developed a number of rather fanciful theories about the early phases of Mediterranean history. Even to such "unscientific" historical data as the myth of the lost land of Atlantis, they devoted respectful attention and detailed research. These theories— which in their imaginative audacity so much resembled his own —Spengler sought to systematize and to bring into harmony with his already-established historical scheme.

As the work advanced, it soon became apparent to Spengler that his "metaphysical" search for the original categories of human activity and his newer interest in pre-cultural man were really only two aspects of the same investigation. By 1926, he had fused them into a single draft project, which was subsequently found in his posthumous papers.[22] And during the next decade, the historical aspect of this double undertaking appears gradually to have come to predominate over the philosophical. Finally, in 1935—shortly after the Nazi boycott combined with a slight improvement in his physical condition had led Spengler to return to active historical work—the establishment of a new

[21] Kornhardt, " 'Deutschland in Gefahr,' " p. 6.
[22] On all the above, see Hildegard Kornhardt, " 'Urfragen:' Ein Bericht über den Nachlass Oswald Spenglers," mimeographed, n.d., pp. 1–2.

review gave him a suitable outlet for his researches. It was in *Die Welt als Geschichte* (The World as History), to whose founders Spengler had given a much-appreciated encouragement, that his last fragmentary writings were to appear.

The new review was devoted to questions of "universal history." Thus, although it had only a limited circulation and could reach a public not even remotely approaching that to which Spengler had become accustomed, it at least provided him with the sort of scholarly sympathy that he had lacked nearly all his life. In the first year of its existence, *The World as History* published a sizable chunk of Spengler's essay in pre-history under the title "A Contribution to the World History of the Second Millennium before Christ." This millennium, in Spengler's view, represented a vital turning point in human development. It marked the time when the earliest cultures, those of Egypt and Babylon, were nearing their end, and when three more "northern" cultures —the Classical, the Indian, and the Chinese—were coming to birth. As opposed to their more tranquil predecessors, these new cultures felt life to be a "riddle"—thus posing the problem that has occupied mankind ever since. To investigate so obscure an epoch, Spengler argued, the historian must use all the creative imagination at his disposal. He should not rest content, along with the conventional archaeologists and philologists, to report simply what the existing relics suggested. He must make a mighty effort to see beyond his sources to the final relationships that no merely "systematic" study could reveal.[23]

The published fragment could scarcely satisfy all the expectations aroused by Spengler's announced program. But it at least showed that the author of the *Decline* had returned to his earlier level—that his incomparable historical imagination was again at work. As before, the learned world paid little heed to what he had written. Only a handful of specialists found anything to praise in the "Second Millennium"—among them a certain Finnish student of Cretan inscriptions, who spoke of an "enormous

[23] "Zur Weltgeschichte des zweiten vorchristlichen Jahrtausends" is included in *Reden und Aufsätze*, pp. 158–291.

number of thoughts" that would "surely prove to be very fruit-ful.[24] Other, shorter fragments of Spengler's pre-history were to appear in the same review after his death.[25] But the last words published during his own lifetime were on a totally different theme—a belated, isolated return to his political interests. In early 1936, in answer to a circular question of American origin on the possibilities for world peace, Spengler telegraphed back: "Pacifism will remain an ideal, and war a fact, and if the white peoples are resolved to wage war no more, the colored will do so and will be the rulers of the earth." [26]

In the early morning of May 8, 1936, Spengler died of a heart attack. His sisters buried him quietly, with the request that expressions of sympathy be omitted.

[24] Joh. Sundwall, quoted by Professor Hans Erich Stier, editor of *Die Welt als Geschichte*, in a letter to the author.

[25] The following articles, all of which appeared in *Die Welt als Geschichte* in 1936 and 1937, are included in *Reden und Aufsätze*, under their original dates of composition: "Plan eines neuen Atlas antiquus" (1924), pp. 96–104; "Altasien: Aufgaben und Methoden" (1924), pp. 105–109; "Das Alter der amerikanischen Kulturen" (1933), pp. 138–147; "Der Streitwagen und seine Bedeutung für den Gang der Weltgeschichte" (1934), pp. 148–152.

[26] "Ist Weltfriede möglich?"; *Reden und Aufsätze*, pp. 292–293.

CHAPTER NINE

THE NEW SPENGLERIANS

SPENGLER might well have died in despair. By 1936, his influence had almost disappeared. In Germany, he stood officially condemned as an unwholesome pessimist and reactionary. The national revolution he had predicted and fought for had turned against him. Abroad, he was blamed for helping to power the very regime that in his own country would have none of him. Even in America, where he had found his least critical audience, his doctrines were no longer popular. After 1933, philosophical pessimism had become old-fashioned. With the New Deal, the emphasis had shifted to "social significance" and "constructive" activity. Elsewhere in the West—despite the economic depression—pessimism no longer answered to the prevailing intellectual temper: the struggle against fascism, the organization of Popular Fronts, the hope for peace through collective security—these were the things that occupied the thoughts of those who felt themselves to be in the mainstream of current activity. The decaying West had roused itself from its torpor and would listen no more to the prophet of inevitable decline.

Yet even at the nadir of Spengler's influence the forces were already in the making that a half decade later would restore him to intellectual currency. By 1940, two wholly unrelated developments had brought Spengler again to the attention of a wide public. A new group of cyclical historians had begun to publish their interpretations of Western civilization that necessarily in-

vited comparison with Spengler's own. And the rapid deteriora-
tion of the international outlook culminating in the fall of France
had again provided a justification for pessimistic conclusions.
Both of these developments—in somewhat changed form—have
continued to focus interest on Spengler until the present time.

*   *   *

In the middle and late thirties, two philosophical writers,
one a British historian and the other a Russian sociologist, working independently of Spengler and of each other, brought out a
series of volumes even more comprehensive than the *Decline*.
While their methods and conclusions were unquestionably original, they offered a structure of historical interpretation whose
family resemblance to Spengler's could not fail to strike the most
superficial of readers.

The first of these in date of publication was Arnold Toynbee's *A Study of History*. The first three volumes appeared in
1934, three more in 1939, and the final four—much delayed by
the author's wartime public service—were at last published in
1954. Together they offer the result of a lifetime's labor. For
Toynbee's original rough formulation of his historical scheme
came a full forty years before its completion—and before he
became aware that Spengler was working along parallel lines.
When, in the summer of 1920, Toynbee read the *Decline,* his
first reaction was to wonder whether his "whole inquiry had been
disposed of by Spengler before even the questions, not to speak
of the answers, had fully taken shape" in his own mind. But after
further study, he concluded that on the question of the "geneses
of civilizations" Spengler was "most unilluminatingly dogmatic
and deterministic," and that there was room for "English empiricism" to make a try "where the German *a priori* method drew
blank." [1]

It is a remarkable sign of the contemporary relevance of
cyclical doctrines that two historians of such different tempera-

[1] Arnold J. Toynbee, "My View of History," in *Civilization on Trial* (New
York, 1948), pp. 9–10.

ments and intellectual formations should have arrived virtually simultaneously at similar conclusions. These similarities, however, are more in structure than in philosophical approach. Like Spengler, Toynbee rejects the straight-line succession of ancient, medieval, and modern history, and substitutes for it a study of comparative civilizations. He places a similar emphasis on cultural, as opposed to political or economic history, and on the activities of élites, which he calls "creative minorities." And, like Spengler's, Toynbee's civilizations end as all-embracing empires —in Toynbee's phraseology, "universal states"—which can preserve for an indefinite period the outward forms of a society from which all cultural vitality has departed. Yet even within this historical structure, we find significant differences. Toynbee's cultural emphasis is literary and philosophical, where Spengler's was artistic, and he delimits his civilizations in a more conventional and at the same time more rigorous fashion. Besides adding a number of relatively obscure civilizations that Spengler had either included in the major cultures or neglected entirely, Toynbee refuses to ascribe any unity to the "Magian" world. He separates the history of Byzantium—the "Orthodox Christian" civilization —from that of the Arabs, and returns to the more usual practice of beginning the history of the West with the decline and fall of Rome. The result is a structure of comparative civilizations that strikes us as both more solid and more comprehensive than the one that Spengler had offered.

Such differences, however, are comparatively superficial— a question simply of the way in which the individual historian chooses to divide up or slant his material. Below them, we find a contrast of philosophical orientation that puts Toynbee in sharp opposition to most of Spengler's major tenets. Flexibility, empiricism, a religious and ethical interpretation opening the way to basically optimistic conclusions on the future of the West—all these give Toynbee's work a character of serenity and good temper that is totally lacking in the writings of his German predecessor.

As a far more careful and methodical historian than Speng-

ler, Toynbee combines a respect for the former's imaginative
insight with a vigorous rejection of his dogmatic tone. "Over-
emphasis and hyper-dogmatism," he finds, ". . . is the serious
blemish in Spengler's remarkable work." And he refuses to adopt
in all its literal implications Spengler's biological metaphor of
civilizations as "super-organisms." [2] Hence he denies the existence
of any historical law of inevitable decline: in Toynbee's work
there is no determinism, no fixed life-span for each civilization.
Nor do his civilizations go their ways in strict separation and
mutual incomprehensibility: through "apparentation and affilia-
tion," through the "universal churches" and "internal proleta-
riats" that within an old society establish the philosophic foundations for a new one, most of them are joined by living and
tangible links. Moreover, Toynbee attempts to solve the final and
most difficult problem of the origin of civilization itself: in his
theory of "challenge and response" he proposes an answer to
the question that Spengler had simply left as one of those ultimate
mysteries of "destiny" on which the historian should refrain from
laying his profane and clumsy hand.

Thus Toynbee softens the asperities and opens up the tight
compartments of Spengler's uncompromising structure. Through
the English historian's work, there runs a thread of open-minded-
ness and common sense that keeps him from driving any of his
theories to their extreme conclusions. It is partly this that re-
strains him from passing a final verdict of decline on his own
society. But there is something more important—and in this respect Toynbee displays a greater dogmatism than Spengler himself. Beyond everything else, the thing that distinguishes *A Study
of History* from the *Decline* is that it is written from the standpoint of a Christian believer. As a good Christian, Toynbee cannot at the same time be a historical or ethical relativist. For him,
Christianity and its ethics represent final truth. Hence the history
of the West, since it is primarily the history of organized Christianity, must necessarily be different from that of previous civili-

[2] Arnold J. Toynbee, *A Study of History,* III (Oxford and London, 1934),
pp. 221–222, 378.

zations. Although there may be no law of inevitable decline, all civilizations have in fact declined; Toynbee's historical vocabulary of "birth, growth, and decay" has already implied as much. But the Christian historian can scarcely grant that a civilization which has the unique distinction of serving as the vehicle of the true Church can suffer the fate of its predecessors. Thus Toynbee, although detecting in Western society nearly all the usual symptoms of decay, will not go on to predict its doom. He leaves room for hope—and it is this that largely explains his popularity with a wide segment of readers not ordinarily interested in serious historical writing. Like Spengler, he has come to represent for his admirers not so much an analyst of the past as an inspiring prophet and moral teacher for the future.

In its final form, then, Toynbee's scheme of history is no longer strictly cyclical. Like Joachim's or Vico's, it is a combination of the circle and the straight line in which "the movement of civilizations may be cyclic and recurrent, while the movement of religion may be on a single continuous upward level." [3] Ultimately, the Christian concept of direction wins out over the more static tradition inherited from the ancients.

The second major cyclical work of the thirties departs even more radically than Toynbee's from the classical tradition. Although no apologist for organized religion, Pitirim A. Sorokin, whose four-volume *Social and Cultural Dynamics* was published in the United States between 1937 and 1941, believes at least as strongly as Toynbee in the primacy of spiritual values. Sorokin is not interested in the exact delimitation of specific and self-contained "civilizations." In fact, he appears to doubt their existence. He directs his efforts, rather, toward defining three basic attitudes —the "ideational," the "idealistic," and the "sensate"—that he believes have predominated in fairly uniform succession in the development of recorded societies.

These basic attitudes Sorokin calls "supersystems." Within them, he finds all sorts of smaller systems, ranging from a complete scheme of philosophy down to the most trivial juxtaposi-

[3] Sorokin, *op. cit.*, p. 120.

tions of meaningful statement or activity. Thus Sorokin concentrates on units of study either larger or smaller than Spengler's and Toynbee's cultures or civilizations. As a result his historical scheme is less neat than theirs: the systems and supersystems overlap and intersect each other most bewilderingly in a wide variety of patterns and curves. Part of this diversity is owing to Sorokin's use of statistical measurements to check his more imaginative conclusions. Such a method necessarily produces outlines that are far less satisfying from the aesthetic standpoint than the more symmetrical patterns derived largely from intuition—and this is obviously the origin of Toynbee's as of Spengler's scheme —in which historical data can find secure nesting-places already prepared for them.

Very much the same thing may be said of the work of the American anthropologist Alfred L. Kroeber, whose *Configurations of Culture Growth,* although appearing toward the end of the Second World War, should properly be discussed along with the writings of Toynbee and Sorokin. Like Sorokin, Kroeber interests himself primarily in "fundamental patterns of cultures" and refrains from establishing the precise boundaries between civilizations. Like him, he tries for quantitative measurements based on "clusters" of geniuses at certain historical epochs. And more rigorously than Toynbee or Sorokin, he defines the theories that he shares with Spengler and the points on which he differs. Kroeber finds himself in agreement with the author of the *Decline* in postulating the "existence of certain fundamental patterns characteristic of each major culture" and believing that they "occur in limited growths." But he seeks to establish only their "configurations" in time and space—thereby ruling out the "difficult task of expressing the essential patterns themselves," which, as he sees more clearly than most of his contemporaries, "necessitates an intuitionally subjective approach." Beyond this self-limitation, Kroeber specifically rejects three basic Spenglerian concepts: that a "single master or key pattern" controls each culture; that all cultures develop in parallel stages; and that they "die of themselves." None of these does he reject totally; he simply finds them "wholly unproved." [4] And in general, we may say of Kroeber's book that it is at the same time the most sensible and the least conclusive of the contemporary efforts at historical synthesis. Perhaps these two qualities are inseparable in a task so laden with difficulties—of philosophy, of method, and of basic definition.

Despite such difficulties, Spengler's successors of the thirties and forties—two of whom are still at work today—have performed an extraordinary intellectual function. As one of them has written of his fellows: "Whatever its mistakes . . . , the [cyclical] school does not dodge the truly crucial problems. For this reason even its errors are likely to be more fruitful than the correct trivialities or painfully accurate platitudes of the bulk of the precise 'researches' of today's social and humanistic disciplines." [5] The cyclical theorists have taught a new generation to regard the movement of history around them in a radically different fashion from preceding generations. People now take quite calmly ideas that seemed nothing short of devastating when Spengler originally enunciated them more than forty years ago.

Thus the notion of human development as proceeding in cycles rather than a straight line has become very nearly commonplace. And other ideas that Spengler shares with his successors have gained widespread acceptance: the view of history as a comparative study of civilizations with an equal claim to respectful attention; an analysis of the development of each civilization in terms of growth, maturity, and decay; the assertion that these civilizations start with mystic and heroic values, and, after passing through a major phase of happy harmony between spiritual and intellectual emphases, end in an arid period of materialism and hyper-intellectuality; the view of the present as a "late" epoch in the history of the West—either advanced maturity or decay, depending on the amount of constitutional optimism that the individual writer can muster. Even on such a specific problem as the role of religion in a decaying society, these theorists have

[4] Kroeber, *op. cit.,* pp. 825–828.
[5] Sorokin, *op. cit.,* p. 322.

offered their readers a wide measure of agreement: Toynbee's
"universal church" looks like Spengler's "second religiosity"
turned upside down and reoriented toward a Christian goal. And
Sorokin too has found in a revival of spiritual values new hope
for an aging society. Where Spengler with hostile eyes viewed the
return of religion as the conclusive sign of a descent into formlessness, his successors, as deeply sincere advocates of spiritual
renewal, have hailed it as the salvation of a civilization far gone
in worldliness.

In general, then, the independent restatement of certain
basic Spenglerian concepts in the late thirties pointed to broadly
optimistic conclusions. But these were the product of a *tour de
force*: the logic of the data seemed to point in another direction,
and it was only an act of faith that held them on their upward
course. An unfavorable turn in the course of Western history
could send them scurrying back where Spengler had originally
aligned them.

*   *   *

Since 1940, the course of world events has favored the
propagation of pessimistic doctrines. Aside from the relatively
brief period of Allied victory in the Second World War—the
years 1943 to 1945—the past decades of war and armed truce
have offered few grounds for confidence in the future of the West.
Corresponding to the curve of the permanent international crisis,
to the alternations of hope and despondency that it has provoked,
we find two main periods of renewed interest in Spenglerian
ideas: the years 1940 to 1942, and the period since 1946. As we
might expect, this interest has manifested itself chiefly in Germany and the United States, the countries that had originally
provided Spengler with his most devoted admirers.

The first years of the war saw the publication of two Spenglerian popularizations that frankly attempted to apply to the
events of the hour the words of the *Decline* itself. In America in
1940 Edwin Franden Dakin published a volume of "vital excerpts" from Spengler's major work under the title *Today and*

Destiny. A year later, despite the continued Nazi hostility to Spengler's memory, his German publishers brought out a similar collection. This latter volume was the direct outgrowth of wartime needs. Its original conception came from the letter of a young soldier, who had expressed a desire for a convenient selection of Spenglerian quotations dealing with "deportment" and the maintenance of "form." [6] Faced with the bitter reality of war service, at least one young German—the Nazi illusion of easy triumphs now behind him—was turning to Spengler as a source of moral strength in difficult circumstances. The resulting collection combined quotations from the *Decline* and the political works with gleanings from the unpublished portions of Spengler's "metaphysical" book.

By 1942, on the other side of the Atlantic, a German professor in exile was expressing his dismay that his students, like those he had known in Germany in the 1920's, were buying and reading the *Decline* "without being instructed to do so." And he further noted that the prophets of the "managerial revolution" were drawing on Spengler for inspiration.[7] The mood that so alarmed the scholarly refugee, with his twenty-year perspective of Spenglerian devastation, is a recent memory to many Americans who were students at the time. In the years 1940 and 1941, the young American—confronted with the fall of France, a general wavering of faith in democratic procedures, and the approaching involvement in a war in which he could detect no clear imperative for personal sacrifice—quite naturally turned to pessimistic doctrines.

During the latter part of the war, the American public, caught up in the preoccupations of military activity and systematically warned against the snares of German thinking, had little time for Spengler. By 1946, however, events had again changed for the worse. The growing tension between the Soviet Union and the United States, the collapse of the hope for "One World,"

---

[6] Editor's postscript to *Gedanken,* p. 129.
[7] Hans W. Weigert, "The Future in Retrospect: Oswald Spengler, Twenty-Five Years After," *Foreign Affairs,* XXI, October 1942, pp. 121, 126.

again seemed to mark a downward sweep in the historical cycle. The American reading public was ready to turn, as before, to the rival prophets of cosmic doom and historical salvation.

In the late forties, as in the thirties, the renewed interest in Spengler came as a kind of ricochet effect from other literary enthusiasms. The publication in 1946 of F. S. C. Northrop's *The Meeting of East and West,* and in the following year of the one-volume abridgement of Toynbee's *A Study of History,* provided Americans with new keys to the outside world, and taught them to view the current international impasse in terms of contrasting cultural traditions. Both Northrop and Toynbee brought messages of hope. The former sought to lay the groundwork for a reconciliation of the spiritual values of East and West. The latter found reason to believe that Western civilization could reach the political unity required for common defense through the organization of a new type of "universal state"—a free association of nations. For people desperately seeking reasons for hope, such doctrines as these—despite their rather ethereal nature —seemed to provide the intellectual endorsement of scholarship and philosophy. This was true of the bulk of the American reading public, which manifested for Toynbee's work an enthusiasm that the *Decline* even in its best days had never enjoyed. A minority, however, dissatisfied with the optimistic interpretations that seemed to gloss over so much that was disquieting, turned back to Spengler for a more austere message. Again the students, unbidden by their elders, began to plunge into the dark waters of the *Decline.* What they chiefly sought was enlightenment on the sources of conflict between Russia and the West—and the related problem of leadership in the future Western imperium.

In Germany also, where, after remaining for ten years out of print, the *Decline* was at length reissued in 1950, the new student generation, with even more pressing insistence, searched Spengler's utterances for answers to the same agonizing questions. It was only natural that Germans should return to the doctrine of a general *Untergang* now that a catastrophe without precedent in history had overwhelmed their own country. "In a truly demoniacal fashion, the maturing reality and its recognition are here linked together as with no other people since the time of Amos and Isaiah. This fateful entanglement . . . gives Spengler's work its unique meaning for German readers as against analogous works from abroad." [8]

*　　*　　*

We have seen that Spengler agreed with Danilevsky in viewing Russia as a nation whose common history with the West was forced and artificial and whose true history lay in the future. At some not too distant time, they agreed, Russia would create a civilization of her own. But where Danilevsky was happily confident that this would very shortly come about, Spengler was hesitant and uncertain. The future that Danilevsky greeted with joy, the author of the *Decline,* as a loyal son of the West, could only view with foreboding. It was doubtless for this reason that Spengler never predicted in unequivocal terms that the successor culture to the Faustian would arise in Russia—"somewhere in the plains between the Vistula and the Amur." [9] He never wrote the chapter entitled "Russia and the West" that he had announced in 1918 as the concluding section of his forthcoming second volume, and his statements on Russian culture remained in elliptical and fragmentary form.

Nevertheless, in certain passages of the *Decline,* and more particularly in his subsequent lectures and political tracts, Spengler sketched with a fair degree of consistency the outlines of a prediction. The basic symbol of the Russian soul he defined as a

---

[8] Manfred Schroeter, *Metaphysik des Untergangs: Eine kulturkritische Studie über Oswald Spengler* (Munich, 1949), p. 253. It is significant that after a gap of nearly a quarter of a century, Schroeter returned to his study of Spengler at the end of the Second World War. For other examples of the renewed interest in things Spenglerian, see the general cultural history by F. Adama van Scheltema, *Die geistige Mitte: Umrisse einer abendländischen Kulturmorphologie* (Munich, 1947), and the publication of material from Spengler's posthumous papers by Hildegard Kornhardt and Franz Tietze: "Aus dem Nachlass Oswald Spenglers," *Hamburger Akademische Rundschau,* 3. Jahrgang, 3.–6. Hefte, 1948/49, pp. 209–214, 301–308, 473–476.

[9] *Man and Technics,* p. 78.

"plane without limit"—reflecting an ethic of undifferentiated brotherhood. But this symbol had as yet found "no sure expression either in religion or in architecture." The slumbering Russian world-feeling still awaited its unfolding—an unfolding that would manifest itself in the birth of a new religion. Dostoyevsky had been its first great prophet, and its political expression would be "some sort of new Tsarism." [10]

Hence the Bolshevik Revolution could not be taken as the birth of the true Russian culture. It was simply another example of the forced imposition of a Western ideology on an uncomprehending Russian peasantry. Yet not entirely—Bolshevism, Spengler argued, had a "double meaning." Although itself an alien importation, it had destroyed the original foreign structure—the regime established by Peter the Great—and in so doing had opened the way to the foundation of an indigenous Russian culture. "Under new leaders" it was possible that Bolshevism itself might "change in this direction." But Spengler did not think it likely.[11]

By 1924, however, another sort of change had already set in. With the death of Lenin, Spengler found—somewhat earlier, perhaps, than most of his contemporaries—Russia had begun a return to Asia. Lenin himself had become a "Caesar-figure, the most important since Rhodes." And under his successor—as Spengler noted, with characteristic hyperbole, in his last political work—Russia had ceased to be a state; it had fallen prey, as in the time of the Mongols, to the rule of a barbarian "horde, called the Communist Party, with its chieftains and almighty Khan."

This change might or might not mean the birth-throes of a new religion. Only the distant future could give any hint as to that. But for the immediate present, Spengler argued, Russia offered a very real and practical threat. In returning to Asia it had taken its place alongside the "colored" nations hammering

[10] *Decline,* I, 201; "Preussentum und Sozialismus," *Politische Schriften,* p. 102.
[11] "Das Doppelantlitz Russlands und die deutschen Ostprobleme" (lecture dating from 1922), *Politische Schriften,* pp. 121, 123.

at the bastions of the West. Russia belonged to the enemy. The problem for the Faustians was an elemental matter of self-defense —and Spengler warned more than once against the folly of a preventive attack against the Russian heartland; "this mightiest of the earth's inland areas," he maintained, "is unassailable from outside." [12]

Yet even the more modest task of defending the Western world offered unprecedented difficulties. "The . . . Roman Empire was an enclosed area with frontiers that could be guarded. The position of the present *Imperium* of the white nations, which embraces the whole globe and *includes* the coloured races, is far more difficult." [13] Obviously, a mere league, a free association of nations, would prove inadequate for the task: all such notions Spengler dismissed with scorn as the wishful imaginings of sentimental internationalists. Some one nation must organize a Western empire on the Roman model.

We have seen that Spengler hoped this chosen nation would be his own. Three years after his death, however, the Third Reich plunged the Western world into the greatest of its wars—a war that at length brought the German people to total defeat and foreign occupation. We shall never know whether Spengler would have considered that by this act—which he almost certainly would have condemned as utter madness—Germany had forfeited her claims to leadership. But at least we can assert that such is the view of most present-day Europeans who think in Spenglerian terms. The neo-Spenglerians now look to the United States to organize the Western imperium.

In a few passages of the *Decline,* Spengler revealed a rather uneven acquaintance with the details of American history. To such problems as the logistics of the Civil War—a favorite subject with German military theorists—and the American tradition of constitution-worship, he devoted a sprinkling of pungent side-

[12] "Neue Formen der Weltpolitik" (lecture dating from 1924), *Politische Schriften,* p. 177; "Neubau des Deutschen Reiches," *Politischen Schriften,* p. 294; *Hour of Decision,* p. 61.
[13] *Ibid.,* p. 208.

remarks.[14] Yet he never really understood the United States, nor was he particularly interested in learning more about it. His final verdict on America offered a disconcerting mixture of insight and fancy:

Is the United States a power with a future? . . .

All we know is that so far there is neither a real nation nor a real State. . . . The American does not talk of State or Mother Country . . . but of "*this* country." Actually what it amounts to is a boundless field and a population of trappers, drifting from town to town in the dollar-hunt, unscrupulous and dissolute; for the law is only for those who are not cunning or powerful enough to ignore it.

The resemblance to Bolshevik Russia is far greater than one imagines. There is the same breadth of landscape, which firstly, by excluding any possibility of successful attack by an invader, consequently excludes the experience of real national danger, and, secondly, by making the State not indispensable, prevents the development of any true political outlook. Life is organized exclusively from the economic side and consequently lacks depth. . . . And there is the same dictatorship there as in Russia (it does not matter that it is imposed by society instead of a party), affecting everything . . . that in the Western world is left to the option of individuals. There is one standardized type of American, and, above all, American woman, in body, clothes, and mind. . . . Finally, there is an almost Russian form of State socialism or State capitalism, represented by the mass of trusts, which, like the Russian economic administrations, systematically standardize and control every detail of production and marketing. These are the real lords of the land in both cases. . . .[15]

Spengler never specifically answered the question with which he started this long digression. But obviously he was unim-

[14] *Decline,* II, 421, 430 *n.*
[15] *Hour of Decision,* pp. 67–68.

pressed with the United States as a nation. Indeed, in his sense of the term, it was not yet a nation at all. During his lifetime he would certainly not have supported any American claim to world leadership.

Yet his attitude toward the United States was not wholly negative. He admired the Americans for their technical and industrial proficiency, finding in it a kind of "Roman" quality. And he called his readers' attention to the "striking similarity of many Roman portrait-busts to the matter-of-fact modern heads of the American style." Today, he might find that the Americans, like the Romans before them, were being "seized and pushed" by circumstances, against their will, into an imperial role.[16]

Or he might argue, along with certain Germans and Americans of the present time, that a combination of their two nations should lead the embattled West—the United States to supply the money and the technology, the Germans the soldiers and the Caesars. In some such solution he might find a realistic adjustment to the new circumstances created by the Second World War. Spengler is not here to reply for himself. The question must remain unanswered—in that realm of "mystery" in which the author of the *Decline* was only too happy to let "destiny" promulgate for the future its irrevocable and unfathomable decrees.

[16] *Decline,* I, 358 *n.*; II, 422.

CHAPTER TEN

SPENGLER AND HIS DETRACTORS

WHEN we come to estimate Spengler's significance in the intellectual history of our century, we must recognize at the start that from the standpoint of pure theoretical distinction he is obviously a figure of second rank. He is not one of the great creative intellects of contemporary social thought. Nor is his writing of a comparable quality with that of a Pareto, a Bergson, or a Sorel. But at the same time Spengler occupies a curiously central position. He stands at the convergence of a variety of contrasting—and sometimes contradictory—intellectual strands. Hence the bizarre combination of influences that appear in his work: Romanticism, positivism, historical scepticism, and the dynamism of eternal flux. Spengler never reconciled the contradictions in his intellectual makeup—and apparently felt it unnecessary to do so.

In much that he wrote we see the characteristic mark of the conservative and incompletely educated German intellectual. Against the French, against the powers of "money," he manifested as uncritical a series of prejudices as any lower middle-class German with no claim to cultural attainment. His hatred of democracy, of Marxian socialism, of internationalism displayed its emotional origin at every turn. In his intellectual limitations, he was himself an example of that "civilization" phase whose coming he so tellingly described.[1] Yet with these quite ordinary

[1] Thomas Mann, "Über die Lehre Spenglers" (1924), in *Bemühungen: Neue Folge der Gesammelten Abhandlungen und kleinen Aufsätze* (Berlin, 1925), p. 247.

prejudices he combined a rare ability to see things in the large. Indeed, his very limitations sometimes aided him. As a thinker living in the twilight of the intellectual *demi-monde,* Spengler could dare to say things that a more "respectable" writer would not have risked getting caught on. Spengler had the courage to take tremendous chances—and he has been paying for them ever since.

At the start of this study, we distinguished the various roles in which Spengler would appear—as historian, as diagnostician, as prophet, and as symptom of his time. In the course of our analysis, we have tried to point out in which guise he was figuring at each particular moment of his literary career. But in nearly every case we were obliged to conclude that he was playing at least two roles at once. In the end, it proved impossible to keep these aspects of his thought apart. Ultimately we must assess Spengler in his total intellectual impact. And when we do this, we find that it was as a cultural prognosticator of high intuitive endowment—an observer with a unique talent for catching the essential quality of historical movements and bringing them together in exciting and suggestive new combinations—that he made his permanent contribution. And it is in this capacity that we must confront him with his critics.

*   *   *

Even if we omit all questions of historical detail, we find that the number of major criticisms that may quite cogently be advanced against Spengler's work piles up to a staggering total. Obviously the *Decline* reeks with unpardonable exaggerations, delivered in a tone of dogmatic certainty. Such was the best way, Spengler apparently felt, to shock his readers into intellectual subservience. His whole "morphological" method, as we have more than once observed, is simply an elaborate expansion of a metaphor drawn from biology. As a figure of speech, it has many descriptive advantages. But treated as anything more than that, it becomes a catastrophic limitation on the necessary flexibility of historical thinking. Similarly with the idea of a basic symbol.

Such a symbol, as one of Spengler's successors has very justly observed, cannot stand as a "major premise" to be defined in logically rigorous terms.[2] It can be no more than a vague feeling for the *quality* of a culture—a suggestion for understanding and appreciation, nothing more. If we want to get some good out of Spengler, we should be careful to take neither his morphological method nor his basic symbols too literally. Indeed, they are not essential to his historical scheme. As the example of Toynbee has shown, it is possible to work out the whole theory of comparative civilizations—of their rise, glory, and decline, and the prospects they suggest for our own future—without explicit resort to either of these intellectual constructions.

Nor is Spengler's determinism a necessary or profitable historical position. Philosophically, the problem is insoluble: metaphysicians and theologians have suffered inconclusive agonies over the question of free will since at least the time of St. Augustine. And, surprisingly enough, despite his dogmatic tone, Spengler himself does not adopt an entirely consistent position. Elements of both personal will and irrevocable fate enter into it:

> Spengler . . . is far from accepting with classical detachment the inescapable fate of decline. He challenges those who cherish illusions and, like Nietzsche, teaches them that they should will and love fate, even promote and fulfil it. No ancient ever fancied that the fate of decline should be willed and chosen; for fate is either really fate, and then it is futile to decide upon it, or it is a self-chosen destiny, and then it is no unavoidable fate. Spengler does not solve this problem of natural fate and historical destiny. His pathos grows from the confusion of the will to a future, still open to possibilities, with the acceptance of a definite outcome.[3]

Thus even Spengler cannot escape the human will, which he, like Nietzsche and Schopenhauer before him, finds to be of the very essence of Faustian man. Whatever the arguments, whatever the logic on either side, we Westerners simply refuse to accept the

[2] Sorokin, *op. cit.*, p. 210.   [3] Löwith, *op. cit.*, p. 12.

determinism of inevitable decline. Our historians call it unscientific—the public finds it depressing. And here again, Spengler's major argument can get along without it. To make his point, all he needs to say is that present signs—by analogy with roughly comparable situations in the past—point to cultural sterility, war, and dictatorship. In such a fashion the most modest and conscientious economist—without the remotest intention of "determining" the future—might draw attention to the warning signals of a business depression. If we are wise, we shall go no farther than this in incorporating Spengler's predictions into our own thought. We shall simply use them as guideposts—bright beacons that may help us to imagine the sort of world in which our old age (if we are granted an old age) may be passed.

If we descend to the more specific aspects of Spengler's thought, we shall find that his views conflict at numerous points with the basic postulates of at least five major fields of study. Philosophers have never taken his metaphysics seriously: except as a critique of positivist method, Spengler's metaphysical passages are without value; they achieve the not unusual combination of being murky and superficial in the same breath. Anthropologists reproach him with an ignorance of the very nature of primitive societies, which he describes as essentially without culture. To an economist, Spengler's "understanding of economic events remains that of a helpless dilettante." Trapped within his monomania about the "omnipotence of money," he fails to appreciate the crucial role of the productive process at the base of economic life. "He is so fascinated by the façade of money, by the 'symbolic power' of money, that he turns the symbol into the thing itself." [4] Thus he is led to violate his own principle of never ascribing events to a single "cause." The psychological effects of modern economic life—its devastation of human individuality—Spengler grasps with characteristic "physiognomic" insight. Indeed, this is the most important, if largely unexpressed, implication of his *Man and Technics*. But the workings of the economic process escape him.

[4] Adorno, *op. cit.*, p. 125.

To students of politics, as we have already observed, Spengler can offer very little that is truly original. Moreover, his violent prejudices becloud his whole political outlook. No theorist, of course, can entirely rise above his prejudices: certain preconceptions, certain deeply-held personal attitudes, recognized or implicit, will necessarily penetrate everything he writes. But there are preconceptions that are broad and suffused with human sympathy, and there are others that are narrow and hateful. Spengler's are of the latter variety. They arise from a "contempt of mankind," an invariable sympathy with the rulers rather than the ruled.[5] Moreover, in its old-fashioned conservatism, the basis of Spengler's political thought is simply unrealistic. His neo-feudal nostalgia for "soil" and tradition, his admiration for men "of race" and for an "old polite society," set up a mighty barrier against an understanding of present-day conditions. And they conflict with his own dictum that a "late" society is by very necessity democratic. The major conservative thinkers of our century —the sceptics and the proto-fascists—have in this respect seen more clearly than Spengler. They have recognized—as Spengler himself is able to do when he confines himself to historical diagnosis—that far from restoring aristocratic "form," contemporary conservatism finds its logical end in the vulgar combination of police power and class rule that we have come to call fascism. It was no democratic or liberal principle that prevented Spengler from being a good fascist; it was a combination of personal fastidiousness and political illusion.

Finally, for historians of all schools, certain of Spengler's basic theories are at variance with canons of interpretation enjoying nearly universal acceptance. It would be difficult for any historian to endorse Spengler's practice of forcing his material to fit his predetermined scheme, and his definition of cultures as freestanding and mutually incomprehensible. And—as Spengler himself almost seems to recognize when he emphasizes the unprecedented difficulties of defending the Faustian world—most present-day historians would find our Western society different

---

[5] *Ibid.*, pp. 120–121.

from all its predecessors in that its influence extends to every corner of the earth. These modifications do not touch the center of Spengler's interpretation—but they severely limit its scope and dogmatic rigor.

To such general criticisms, the historical idealists add a further corrective that is extremely telling. They detect in the work of Spengler and his kind a "confusion between a natural process, in which the past dies in being replaced by the present, and an historical process, in which the past, so far as it is historically known, survives in the present." In protesting against a method whereby the "idea of historical process as a mental process . . . is elaborately denied," the historical idealists arrive at the crux of the whole issue.[6] History, they insist, is a subjective matter. It is a mental construction of the individual historian who strives to recreate a living idea of the past in the present. And the theory of the rise and fall of civilizations—the very definition and outline of these civilizations—is as subjective as everything else.

From this standpoint, the cyclical view of history loses its aura of certainty. It becomes simply another method—and an exceedingly fallible one—for establishing the data of history in meaningful outline. As R. G. Collingwood has most judiciously expressed it:

> In this condition, we see history split up into disconnected episodes, each episode forming a relatively intelligible whole, separated from its neighbours by dark ages. . . . Each period with which we are tolerably acquainted, each period which we understand well enough to appreciate the problems and motives of its agents, stands out as something luminous, intelligible, rational and therefore admirable. But each period is an island of light in a sea of darkness. If we ask why it arose out of barbarism, and why it relapsed into barbarism, we cannot answer; and the reason is that if we knew enough to answer the question we should cease to ask it; for if we knew exactly how the Roman Em-

[6] Collingwood, *Idea of History*, pp. 182, 225.

pire (for instance) declined and fell, what it changed into
and how, then . . . the light of our own historical knowledge
would have illuminated the Dark Ages and they would no
longer appear as dark. . . .

The cyclical view of history is thus a function of the
limitations of historical knowledge. Everyone who has any
historical knowledge at all sees history in cycles; and those
who do not know the cause think that history is really built
thus. When they come to settle the exact position and rhythm
of the cycles, no two exactly agree; though a certain measure
of agreement is found among contemporaries, owing to the
fact that the historical knowledge of a given generation . . .
is to a great extent common property. . . .

. . . Some system of cycles there must always be for
every historical student, as every man's shadow must fall
somewhere on his own landscape; but as his shadow moves
with every movement he makes, so his cyclical view of history will shift and dissolve, decompose and recompose itself
anew, with every advance in the historical knowledge of the
individual and the race.[7]

Thus the cyclical interpretation—whether Spengler's or any
other writer's—is subject to constant change. Each generation,
each individual, will set up the cycles differently. But at least this
much is definite. For the past two generations, for the early and
mid-twentieth century, the cyclical approach has proved to be
particularly rewarding. It has appeared to explain more things
than the straight-line interpretation with which earlier generations tried to express the meaning of history. In the pragmatic
test, the cyclical method has gradually been gaining ground.

Our final criterion of judgment, then, is both subjective and
pragmatic. We have stripped Spengler of his determinism, of his
morphological hocus-pocus, of his symbol-worship and his pretensions to competence in philosophy and economics. We have
tried to expose the ugliness of his political prejudices and the way

[7] Collingwood, "Theory of Historical Cycles: II," pp. 445–446.

in which many of his theories violate the basic principles of historical study. And we have redefined in subjective terms the whole notion of historical cycles. It may seem that we have left very little standing. But actually the core of Spengler's interpretation remains intact. In the ultimate test we shall find that the author of the *Decline* can take a quite surprising revenge on his critics and competitors.

*   *   *

Spengler's successors as cyclical theorists have based their work on philosophical presuppositions radically different from his. All of them regard their intellectual constructions as "scientific"—that is, having some claim to objective validity. In their selection and evaluation of data, they have conscientiously tried to apply the recognized canons of scientific method, and they are convinced that their conclusions represent a fair approximation of the "truth." Nor do they adopt the more pragmatic, experimentalist definition of science—the notion of truth as an effective guide to action based on an average of long experience—to which so many contemporary historians and sociologists adhere. Both Sorokin and Kroeber apparently regard their conclusions as having something more than a merely experimental validity. In this sense, they are both positivists. And the same is basically true of Toynbee—although in his case the question is complicated by his apparent hesitation between writing "scientific" history and writing a history of salvation.

In contrast to these three, the *Decline* makes no claim to scientific validity. For Spengler, the essence of history remains a mystery. The best the historian can hope for is through the construction of inspired metaphors to catch a reflection of the ultimate truth that will always elude him. In history, Spengler affirms, we do not ask, as in natural science, whether a theory is true or false: we ask simply whether it is "profound" or "superficial." The distinction is approximately the same as the contrast we have already observed between the "systematic" and "physiognomic" approaches. In Spenglerian terms, all of his successors

may be described as systematic writers; he alone follows the physiognomic method.

Yet the distinction is not quite so clear-cut as that. It holds
only when Spengler is at his most consistent—when he is being
true to the sceptical implications of his own thought. At other
times, the positivist remainder in his intellectual heritage leads
him to make assertions of a totally opposite character. To be
consistent with his own philosophic approach, even Spengler's
determinism should be phrased in subjective terms: it should not
go beyond the statement that to a historian writing in Germany in
the second decade of the twentieth century, it appeared that certain past developments could have happened in no other fashion,
and that a certain succession of future events was inescapable.
But from time to time Spengler implies much more than that: he
leaves his readers with the impression that things actually *happened* as he said they happened, and that the future *must* be as he
said it would be. When Spengler writes in this fashion, he is even
more positivist than his positivist competitors, since he is more
dogmatic.

But at other times, Spengler quite clearly limits the range of
his own omniscience. He recognizes that the validity of his theoretical scheme cannot transcend the historical circumstances of
its composition. "Every living perception," he writes, "including
the one I have proposed, belongs to one single time." And in
asserting the "truth" of what he has discovered, he claims no
more than that it is *"true for me,* and as I believe, true for the
leading minds of the coming time; not true in itself as dissociated
from the conditions imposed by blood and by history, for that is
impossible." [8] He will not quite say that it is all simply his own
personal idea. But he limits himself to the assertion that his theories peculiarly fit the intellectual temper of the present time and
that future thinkers will more and more be led to adopt them.
And this latter claim has found some substantiation in the surprising uniformity with which subsequent cyclical theorists have
developed ideas roughly paralleling those of the *Decline.* When

[8] "Pessimismus?"; *Reden und Aufsätze,* p. 69; *Decline,* I, xiii.

he writes in this fashion, Spengler is actually more modest than his successors, however much the hesitancy and reasonableness of their literary tone may contrast favorably with his. At his most consistent, Spengler is more sceptical than they are, and more sophisticated in his use of historical terminology. His relativist method penetrates more radically and responds more closely to the contemporary demand for critical detachment. This is the guise in which Spengler can best present his own case for continued intellectual currency.

Considered in this light, Spengler's view of the cyclical historian's role appears better thought-out than that of his successors. It would be difficult for any critically-minded historian—whether positivist, idealist, or simple sceptic—to accept the very notion of a scientific cyclical theory. Or at least he could accept it only if he were to define the word "scientific" in contemporary pragmatic terms. Yet no one to date appears to have ventured to construct a cyclical theory on these premises. This reluctance is more than accidental: temperamentally and by the very nature of his method, a pragmatist would find himself at a loss to elaborate an all-inclusive theory of history. His whole emphasis on plural explanations and on attacking each problem on its own merits, would preclude the attempt. Almost inevitably, then, cyclical history falls either into the positivist or into the relativist-mystical category—or into personal combinations of the two. These two attitudes alone appear to offer the requisite dosage of temerity or imaginative scepticism. The middle position that to most contemporary social scientists might seem the most sensible, simply fails to figure in the problem.

Hence it is not going too far to state that the cyclical theories devised up to the present time are all highly personal constructions, based on uncertain and ill-defined criteria of analysis, and having their origin in intuition. They can be called scientific under none of the usual definitions of that term. As Kroeber, alone of Spengler's successors, has recognized, a general theory of history can attain the required degree of systematic precision only on narrow and detailed questions, where some sort of quantitative measurement is possible. Yet even here the selection of evidence injects a huge element of personal arbitrariness and fallibility. If this is so, then obviously the large and really interesting questions fall entirely outside the sphere of the scientific method. On them, the individual historian's creative imagination holds virtually unlimited sway.

Ultimately, then, we may conclude that all cyclical theorists, whether or not they lay claim to scientific validity, play the role of intuitive seers. They are all doing what Spengler alone quite frankly says he is doing. If we decide to adopt this attitude toward them, then we shall judge them far differently from the way in which they have generally been judged up to now. We shall worry far less about the mistakes, the irritating dogmatism, of a writer like Spengler than we should do if we imagined that he and his kind were about to deliver themselves of some sort of final truth. We shall discount his errors and try to appreciate the positive suggestions he can offer. In fact, once we have adopted such an attitude of radical scepticism, we may learn to esteem and relish even the dogmatism of Spengler's utterance. Since we shall not take what he says too literally, we may find that the very intemperance of his statements enhances their imaginative impact.

From this standpoint, we may take our choice of the cyclical constructions on frankly non-scientific grounds. We may judge them first as literature, as imaginative creations, second as prophecies of varying degrees of discernment. On both these grounds, Spengler comes off rather well.

As literature, the *Decline* is without equal in the field of cyclical writing. Spengler's pictorial, figurative language, his talent for finding the images and personalities that set off in high relief an entire epoch of the past—these give to his work a character of excitement, of tension, and of evocative melancholy. He is a master of the telling epithet, of contrasts epitomized in a single abstract noun, of the alternation of involved, architectural sentences with the short hammer blows of unqualified assertion. In its final form the *Decline* becomes the elaborate reconstruction of a vision, a series of "perspectives"—as Spengler himself puts it

—shot boldly into the past and future. Even for those who do not choose to follow them to their ultimate conclusions, these perspectives may illuminate the understanding and offer guidance for fresh investigation. The "Magian" culture may never have existed—but we may use the concept to deepen our imaginative comprehension of a variety of seemingly unrelated manifestations in the art and religion of the Mediterranean world. True or false, such creations as these have permanently enriched our understanding of our past and of our future.

It is not true, as Spengler once boasted, that he had been proved mistaken "on no essential point." [9] Two at least of his predictions have quite obviously failed to materialize. In Western Europe, parliamentary institutions—despite signs of advanced anemia—have to date continued to function. And the major armies of the world have not reduced themselves to small, supranational, strictly personal followings; they are still combinations of mass and professional forces, finding their indispensable support in the patriotic sentiments and industrial productivity of national populations. Here and there, however, bands of expatriated mercenaries, inspired with the desperation of permanent exile from their own country, such as General Anders' Poles of the Second World War and Chiang Kai-shek's Chinese of today, have offered a preliminary view of what may prove to be the new model. These things may be still in the future. But in more general terms we may conclude that Spengler's failure to establish a number of vital links in the sequence of future events reflects the inadequacy of his personal preconceptions. His faulty economics, his "metaphysical" and unrealistic definition of social classes, drastically limit his comprehension of twentieth-century political movements. As a result, his notion of Caesarism remains too much a matter of mere personal leadership to embrace in its entirety the contemporary phenomenon of totalitarianism.

Yet, as with the overwhelming majority of the predictions in the *Decline,* the basic idea is there even when the formulation is faulty. More poignantly than any of his successors, Spengler has

[9] Preface to *Politische Schriften,* p. v.

sensed the unprecedented character of our time—the resurgence
of those primitive values that so sharply divide the twentieth century from the centuries that went before it. This feeling for essen-
tials extends even to his less fortunate utterances. Under the crude
phraseology of a "colored peril," for example, Spengler expresses
something of the tragic cultural misunderstanding between Asia
and the West—an incompatibility far transcending the clash of
political institutions and economic interests. And beyond this
inter-continental struggle, he sees the terrible outlines of a whole
world delivered over to conquest and virtually perpetual war. He
depicts the coming of an age of iron in which the traditional
political issues, having lost any contemporary relevance, will have
reduced themselves to a simple choice between technical expedients. He grasps the dilemma of creative endeavor in an era of
mass culture—its fatal division between a merely repetitive popular art and the esoteric experiments of the "progressive" schools.
And he understands the implications of mass culture itself. He
sees what one of his German critics (using the American expression) calls the whole "phonyness" of contemporary life—the depressing uniformity of great city society and its deadening effect
on democratic procedures.[10] Finally, he comprehends the empti-
ness and despair that are leading so many of our contemporaries
—the untutored and the highly sophisticated alike—to seek solace
in a return to dogmatic religion.

Spengler's talent as an imaginative writer, however, and the
accuracy of his major predictions do not exhaust, or even properly establish, his intellectual importance. It is somewhere between literature and prophecy that the *Decline* has made its most
telling contribution. It is as symptom, as synthesis, as symbol of
a whole age that Spengler's book remains one of the major works
of our century. Indeed it has gained in stature as the passage of
time has enabled us to place it in the context of the events of the
past four decades and the further catastrophes that nearly all of
us anticipate. For when everything else has been said, the *Decline*
bulks largest as the massive concretization of a state of mind—

[10] Adorno, *op. cit.*, p. 119.

the state of mind of an old society anticipating its end. And this —despite brief flurries of hope—has become the characteristic attitude of social observers and the general public alike, both in Europe and, more recently, in the United States. Hence, as imaginative literature, if not as history in the strict sense, *The Decline of the West* offers the nearest thing we have to a key to our times. It formulates more comprehensively than any other single book the modern *malaise* that so many feel and so few can express. It has become the classic summary of the now familiar pessimism of the twentieth-century West with regard to its own historical future.

Together Spengler's predictions, and the state of mind they express, set before us the emergence of a new barbarism. In them, we have learned to recognize our own era.

CHRONOLOGY

1880—Born at Blankenburg, in the Harz, Germany.

1904—Received his doctor's degree from the University of Halle.

1908—Received a teaching appointment in a Hamburg *Realgymnasium*.

1911—Gave up teaching career; moved to Munich.

1918—Published the first version of *The Decline of the West*.

1919—The "Spengler year;" published *Prussianism and Socialism*.

1924—Year of political lectures; made trip to Sweden, Finland, and the Baltic states.

1927—Suffered slight stroke; beginning of period of ill health.

1933—Published *The Hour of Decision*; Nazi boycott of his works.

1935—Began publishing historical fragments in *Die Welt als Geschichte*.

1936—Died in Munich.

SELECTIVE BIBLIOGRAPHY

I. By Spengler

Der Untergang des Abendlandes: Umrisse einer Morphologie der Weltgeschichte; I: *Gestalt und Wirklichkeit* (Munich, 1923); II: *Welthistorische Perspektiven* (Munich, 1922). Translated by Charles Francis Atkinson as *The Decline of the West*; I: *Form and Actuality* (New York, 1926); II: *Perspectives of World-History* (New York, 1928).

Der Mensch und die Technik: Beitrag zu einer Philosophie des Lebens (Munich, 1931); translated by Charles Francis Atkinson as *Man and Technics: A Contribution to a Philosophy of Life* (New York, 1932).

Jahre der Entscheidung: Deutschland und die weltgeschichtliche Entwicklung (Munich, 1933); translated by Charles Francis Atkinson as *The Hour of Decision: Part One: Germany and World-Historical Evolution* (New York, 1934).

Politische Schriften (Political Writings) (Munich, 1932).
Contains "Prussianism and Socialism" (1919), "Reconstruction of the German Reich" (1924), and miscellaneous political lectures.

Reden und Aufsätze (Speeches and Essays) (Munich, 1937).
Contains "Heraclitus" (1904), "Pessimism?" (1921), "A Contribution to the World History of the Second Millennium before Christ" (1935), and other miscellaneous writings.

Gedanken (Thoughts), Hildegard Kornhardt, ed. (Munich, 1941).

A collection of aphorisms, drawn both from Spengler's published works and from his posthumous papers.

"Aus dem Nachlass Oswald Spenglers," Hildegard Kornhardt and Franz Tietze, ed., *Hamburger Akademische Rundschau*, 3. Jahrgang, 3.–6. Hefte, 1948/49, pp. 209–214, 301–308, 473–476.
   Material from Spengler's posthumous papers.

II. On Spengler

Theodor W. Adorno, "Spengler nach dem Untergang: Zu Oswald Spenglers 70. Geburtstag" (Spengler after the Collapse: For Oswald Spengler's 70th Birthday), *Der Monat*, 2. Jahrgang, May 1950, pp. 115–128.
   A contemporary reevaluation.

August Albers, "Oswald Spengler," *Preussische Jahrbücher*, CLXXXXII, 2. Heft, May 1923, pp. 129–137.
   A biographical account by a close friend.

R. G. Collingwood, "Oswald Spengler and the Theory of Historical Cycles," *Antiquity: a Quarterly Review of Archaeology*, I, September 1927, pp. 311–325.
   A highly-critical analysis from a neo-idealist standpoint.

André Fauconnet, *Un Philosophe allemand contemporain: Oswald Spengler* (Paris, 1925).
   A literary and philosophical analysis.

Eduard Meyer, *Spenglers Untergang des Abendlandes* (Berlin, 1925).
   A qualified endorsement by a professional historian.

Pietro Rossi, *Lo storicismo tedesco contemporaneo* (Turin, 1956); *Storia e storicismo nella filosofia contemporanea* (Milan, 1960).

Close analyses of contemporary historical thought, establishing Spengler's relationship both to the neo-idealism of Dilthey, Croce, and Meinecke and to the sociological school of Max Weber.

Hans Joachim Schoeps, *Vorläufer Spenglers: Studien zum Geschichtspessimismus im 19. Jahrhundert,* second edition (Leiden, 1955).

A study of two obscure nineteenth-century historical pessimists (Vollgraff and Lasaulx) whom the author treats as Spengler's predecessors.

Manfred Schroeter, *Metaphysik des Untergangs: Eine kulturkritische Studie über Oswald Spengler* (Munich, 1949).

A philosophical study, strongly pro-Spengler; includes, in slightly abridged form, the author's earlier book, *Der Streit um Spengler* (The Spengler Controversy).

Pitirim A. Sorokin, *Social Philosophies of an Age of Crisis* (Boston, 1950).

Compares Spengler's theories with those of Danilevsky, Toynbee, Northrop, Kroeber, and several others.

Ernst Stutz, *Oswald Spengler als politischer Denker* (Bern, 1958).

A careful, if hostile, assessment, arguing a close relationship between Spengler's historical and his political ideas.

Joseph Vogt, *Wege zum historischen Universum: Von Ranke bis Toynbee* (Stuttgart, 1961).

A useful handbook, establishing Spengler's place in the tradition of "universal history" over the past century and a quarter.

APPENDIX I

SPENGLER AND HIS "GERMANIC" COMPETITORS

ONE of the most curious features of Spengler's work is that it makes so little reference to the ideas of nationalist political thinkers whose writings both anticipated and paralleled his own. He refuses to recognize his place in a century-long series of "Germanic" ideologists striving for "the revival of a mythical *Deutschtum* and the creation of political institutions that would embody and preserve" the "peculiar character of the Germans." [1]

Particularly surprising is the fact that nowhere in the *Decline* does Spengler refer to Julius Langbehn's *Rembrandt als Erzieher* (Rembrandt as Educator). This book—anonymously published in 1890—was the first non-fiction best-seller in German publishing history, with total sales that remained unparalleled until Spengler's own book appeared. In other respects also the two works resembled each other: the "Rembrandt-book," as it came to be called, gave premonitions of the *Decline* in its tumultuous display of miscellaneous learning, its portentous and prophetic tone, and its stress on the figurative arts as the symbols and symptoms of cultural crisis. Langbehn's level of education and thought was far below Spengler's: it would not be too unfair to dismiss him as a psychopath and a crank. But he tapped the same public and spoke to the same kind of spiritual *malaise* as the author of the *Decline* a generation later.

[1] Fritz Stern, *The Politics of Cultural Despair* (Berkeley and Los Angeles, 1961), p. xiii.

In the immediate aftermath of the First World War, this sense of spiritual disorientation was almost universal. Neo-conservative publicists, imaginative writers, and academic students of German society alike expressed it in a wide variety of forms. With two of these cultural critics—Max Weber and Moeller van den Bruck—Spengler engaged in formal debate. The exchange with Weber took place in the Munich City Hall during the winter of 1919–1920, when Weber himself had only a few months to live. It lasted a day and a half: a knot of invited scholars spurred on the two main contestants, while a youthful audience of strongly-contrasting political persuasions followed the debate with lively interest. Weber handled his antagonist sparingly and with respect—far more gently than was customary in the German academic world. The author of the *Decline* he considered "a very ingenious and learned dilettant" whom he was happy to meet and whom he subsequently invited to his own house.[2]

The encounter with Moeller van den Bruck, which took place a few weeks later, was before a more aristocratic audience —the Berlin June Club, whose guiding spirit was Moeller himself. Apparently no meeting of minds occurred: "We get the impression of a head-on clash between two winds, a storm of abstract verbiage."[3] Moeller's main count against Spengler was his pessimism about the fate of the West as a whole, which made no distinction between the recent victors and the vanquished. For the "young peoples," for Russia and Germany, Moeller argued, "the outcome of the war had restored the promise of life and growth, had separated them with finality from the decaying West."[4] Yet to one at least in the audience it appeared that the two contestants were not so far apart as they themselves supposed. "The Pessimist and the Optimist of the West" offered conceptions that "were opposed to each other and yet attuned to each other and complementary . . . , so that all of us, moved by this

[2] Marianne Weber, *Max Weber: Ein Lebensbild,* new edition (Heidelberg, 1950), pp. 725–727.
[3] Klemens von Klemperer, *Germany's New Conservatism* (Princeton, 1957), p. 175.
[4] Stern, *op. cit.,* p. 239.

moment, solemnly swore to devote our lives to the realization of these visions." [5] The years that followed were to vindicate such an interpretation: in his subsequent political utterances Spengler moved closer to the hopes for the German people that Moeller voiced in his *Third Reich*.

The same years saw the decisive split in German neo-conservatism. The rationalists and humanists went one way, accepting the Weimar Republic as the best solution that could be had, while the prophets of corporative authoritarianism—Spengler, Moeller, and the others—became increasingly shrill in their denunciations of the Republic and democracy. In actuality, the two groups had never belonged together: men like Weber and Thomas Mann had always been of a radically different temper from the visionaries of a German apocalypse. During and just after the First World War, they had found themselves temporarily in the same camp because they had a common enemy—the regime of William II and the shams it stood for. But they hated it for opposite reasons: those who were later to endorse the Weimar solution condemned the Empire as insufficiently democratic; those who subsequently preached authoritarianism found Wilhelminian rule lacking in true national grandeur. On a number of secondary criticisms the two groups were in agreement. But their basic values had little in common. Men such as Weber and Mann were heirs of the Enlightenment: the logic of the unfolding situation eventually led them to democracy. Spengler and his like were full of hatred and scorn: only very special (and not particularly admirable) reservations held them back from becoming racists and Nazis.

[5] Otto Strasser, *History in My Time* (London, 1941), p. 200, cited by both Klemperer and Stern.

APPENDIX II

MORE "NEW SPENGLERIANS"

URING the decade 1952–1961 there appeared five new works adding significantly to the continuing debate on Spengler's importance as a historian and his place in intellectual history. Two are by Americans, one by a Spaniard, and the final two (including what is apparently Toynbee's last word on the subject) have come from England.

* * *

With Herbert J. Muller's *The Uses of the Past* (New York, 1952), the comparative history of civilizations threatens to become almost too sensible. These "profiles of former societies," as the author sub-titles his work, mark a further stage beyond Toynbee in eroding the sharp edges of Spengler's massive construction. Here the provocative features of the *Decline* have disappeared entirely; in this mid-century version of the familiar cosmic drama, serene reason and good sense, balanced argumentation and Anglo-Saxon empiricism, have expelled the thunders of the melancholy Teuton.

Muller's work is avowedly slighter than those of his predecessors. It is brief—even briefer than D. C. Somervell's abridgment of Toynbee—businesslike, and based almost entirely on secondary works. It makes no claim to original scholarship or even original hypothesis. It is rather a synthesis of what some of the best historical thinkers of the past few decades have contributed to the enlargement of our vision. But it is by no means a mechanical digest. Muller has succeeded in integrating his material in a manner that achieves clarity without sacrificing the complexity of the original thought. His style is careful and usually felicitous; only toward the end of his work does it grow tedious. The result is in its modest way a kind of *summa*.

Thus *The Uses of the Past* has the advantage of its self-limitations. It is not a theory or ordered structure of comparative societies. It is not even an attempt to find "configurations," in Kroeber's sense. It is simply a series of "profiles"—as I understand it, a common denominator of generalizations about a number of societies (Israel, Greece, Rome, Byzantium, the European and American West, Russia, India, and China) sufficiently accepted as such so that they demand no closer definition. Beyond this—and perhaps more significantly—Muller expresses two basic attitudes toward history. The first, a plea for a mixture of "piety" and "irony" and a sense of tragedy in viewing the past, is appealing but not particularly provocative: it is roughly what all the more discerning historians of today believe whether or not they consciously formulate it. The author's second attitude is more controversial: a reassertion of faith in reason and humanism as operating principles both in historical interpretation and, to an extent, in the data of history itself. These two criteria of judgment, which he apparently regards as the implicit presuppositions of Western empirical method, Muller applies to the writings of the twentieth-century historical synthesizers. Hence his work amounts to a post-irrationalist salvage operation directed both at finding out how much can be rescued from the more traditional view of history as the evolution of Western democratic values, and at testing to what extent the largely "intuitive" theories of the historians of comparative civilization can support the test of empirical criticism. It is not surprising that Muller leaves little standing in Spengler's and Toynbee's symmetrical structures. The wonder is how much survives; even Spengler's "Faustian" man emerges nearly intact.

This book comes as a welcome corrective. It is refreshing to see the Enlightenment established once again in the place of honor, to hear the early Middle Ages frankly called "dark," and to read that "man's history on earth still looks like an evolution, and in the long view even like a progress." [1] Yet Muller strives so hard to restore a sense of reasonableness in historical interpretation as against those who see only drift, unreason, and decay, that he says rather more than he needs to. And by the same token he challenges to combat some antiquated windmills. Besides engaging in a running skirmish with Toynbee—definitely no windmill—Muller takes on a number of adversaries unworthy of his pen: worshippers of the Middle Ages, now nearly forgotten, like Ralph Adams Cram, and a variety of literal-minded Christian divines. Moreover, the antiphonal method he adopts in marshalling his material—first the virtues of a society, then its vices—ends in weariness: the literary device is too neat and repetitious. In the showdown, then, for all the gentleness and reasonableness of his tone, Muller proves to be as polemical as his predecessors in the ever-popular pursuit of historical comparisons. If Toynbee has been likened to St. Augustine, Muller may with no greater injustice be compared to Gibbon—a Gibbon chastened by a century and a half of turmoil and disaster, but still girded for battle with the forces of barbarism and religion.

*   *   *

Thirteen years after the publication of his *Configurations of Culture Growth*, Alfred L. Kroeber delineated more precisely his attitude toward Spengler in a series of lectures entitled *Style and Civilizations* (Ithaca, 1957). This final work of Kroeber's old age devotes one full lecture to an analysis of the *Decline* and another to Spengler's predecessors and successors.

In focussing his attention on artistic style, Kroeber finally makes explicit what was only implied in his earlier book—that style is "the most sensitive . . . indicator" for distinguishing civilizations from one another. Here he takes his stand with Spengler, although he is far less confident about how the job is to be done. Dismissing Spengler's biological terminology as in-

[1] p. 367.

appropriate to what he was actually trying to do, Kroeber argues that the real achievement of the *Decline* is to associate "parts of a culture, whose substance and immediate function are highly diverse, but which nevertheless do carry a common quality." He even has a good word for the "prime symbols" that his earlier book severely criticized: the strength of such metaphors as "vaulted cavern" or "unending plane," Kroeber finds, "is proportional to the number and vigor of allusive threads that run out from them into the huge mass of phenomena referred to." Thus Spengler, "in a passionate and tumultuous way," made a conscientious effort to give a "coherent characterization of our civilization"—a task that Kroeber sees as strewn with difficulties but not totally above the analytic capacity of human beings.[2]

Beyond this limited endorsement of Spenglerian method, Kroeber will not go. True to the good sense that has made him both the most generous and the most judicious of Spengler's critics, he again rejects determinism and all accompanying notions of inevitable doom. Our own civilization he finds to be in a state of reorganization "on a broader base, allowing an ultimately wider range of patterns and styles," rather than in a condition of decay or collapse. The comparative study of civilizations, Kroeber concludes, "can hardly become truly scientific or scholarly until it divests itself of emotional concern about crisis, decay, collapse, extinction, and doom." [3]

As Kroeber's last lectures were being delivered, a young English admirer of his was working on a parallel book of "prologomena to the comparative study of civilizations" whose further elaboration was cut short by the author's untimely death. Philip Bagby's *Culture and History* (London, 1958) is both dedicated to Kroeber and inspired by his example. And it is not only as a student of comparative civilizations that Bagby looks to Kroeber for guidance. In his opening chapters he argues that the historical profession as a whole should draw on cultural anthro-

[2] pp. 100–102, 155.
[3] pp. 157, 160.

pology—and hence on the work of men like Kroeber—as "most likely to provide the concepts and methods necessary to illuminate the dark jungle of historical events." [4]

This is a point of view with which I have great sympathy, but I do not think that Bagby has stated his case as competently as he might have done. His prose betrays the stiffness of the very young scholar, and a good deal of his book is occupied with a pedestrian rehearsing of the old saws of contemporary English historical philosophy. He blunders badly in calling Vico a "half-educated Neapolitan literary hack" (a judgment which he appears to reverse in respectful references later in his book); he spins out his arguments to the point of tedium; and his final claim to have "in a sense" reconciled "the idealist and positivist approaches to history," by placing "ideas and values in a central position," while defining them empirically, is simply Max Weber brought up to date and turned onto the field of anthropology.[5] Nevertheless, Bagby's book is important—if only as a summary of what many contemporary historians think and practise, but have not bothered to put on paper.

Like Kroeber, Bagby has some kind things to say about Spengler—far more than about Toynbee, whom he regards as representing "a step backwards towards the pre-scientific moralizing philosophy of history. . . . Spengler, on the other hand, in spite of his wild exaggerations and his reliance on intuition, did have a concept of culture which approaches the anthropological one and used it far more systematically and with far more respect for the evidence than his successor." When he comes to draw up his own roster of civilizations, Bagby arrives at a list closely resembling Spengler's, even finding room for the much-maligned "Magian" construction. Similarly he prefers "Caesarism" to Toynbee's "universal state" as a political characterization of a "late" phase in civilized society. In short, Bagby goes even farther than Kroeber in venturing the guess that "future

[4] p. 71.
[5] pp. 12, 203.

empirical studies . . . will validate some, though . . . certainly not all," of Spengler's conclusions.[6]

Nonetheless, Bagby sticks with Kroeber in not trying to chart an exact course for the rise and fall of civilizations. He merely seeks to define "recurring configurations which we should look for in our comparisons." In so doing, he wants to persuade his fellow-historians that "the comparative study of the development of ideas and values is the key to the understanding of history."

> Although we are likely to find some regularities in the development and inter-relationships of lesser cultural phenomena, these cannot be fully intelligible until we see what regularities may be found in the development of ideas and values. Indeed, it seems probable that the difficulties which have been encountered so far by sociologists and anthropologists in formulating generalizations of universal validity are due in large measure to the fact that they have been looking for them on the wrong level; they have concentrated on the lesser cultural phenomena and neglected the greater.[7]

Such is Bagby's final injunction to the profession. The passage is characteristic of the clarity and force of his thinking. But it also shows the author's limitations. Phrases like "key to the understanding" and "fully intelligible" reveal how Bagby, in common with his master Kroeber, is still in part enmeshed in the formulas and aspirations of nineteenth-century positivism. These two seem to believe that there is such a thing as a "configuration"—a historical or anthropological structure actually existing "out there"—as opposed to a mere perspective on the kaleidoscopic (and subjective) data of human experience; they apparently imagine that in so slippery a field it is possible to arrive at unequivocal conclusions on which "scientific" investigators can agree. In this respect, Kroeber's and Bagby's work derives from the more doubtful and antiquated aspects of Spengler's labors. It

[6] p. 181.
[7] pp. 183, 191.

does not reflect his true stature as a poet of historical interpretation.

*   *   *

Far more perplexing, and with no claim to anthropological or any other kind of scientific competence, is Luis Diez del Corral's *The Rape of Europe* (New York, 1959). On the one hand, it is a work of literary-philosophical speculation, loose in structure, and ranging over the whole course of European history. In this first guise, the author draws on the example of Hegel, Comte, Dilthey, and Ortega—the last of whom is quite evidently his master—and in addition, as a respected precedent for such a venture, on the work of Spengler himself. The method is unashamedly intuitive: his aim, the author tells us, is "to take in a whole panorama, or find the cardinal points in a horizon," to emulate the sort of "visual intelligence that fills the works of a Ranke or a Burckhardt." [8]

At the same time, *The Rape of Europe* rises far above the level of comparable essays on the past and future of Western civilization. The author's learning is enormous: he is equally at home in the classics and in the works of such contemporary American analysts of urban society as Lewis Mumford. And he rejects any notion of tight schematization. His aim, rather, is to capitalize on the unusual perspective offered by Spain to warn his fellow-Europeans of the paradoxical historical fate which they are experiencing, and which Spaniards understand better than the rest, since it hit them earlier.

This fate is metaphorically expressed in the ancient myth of Europa and the bull, and it is under its "invocation" that the author places his book. The contemporary version of the myth runs as follows: Western civilization, the exquisite, unique product of three millennia of slow construction, with its pluralism, its refined articulations, and its tense equilibrium between spiritual and technical concerns—this legacy of an unrepeatable concatenation of historical circumstances has been literally gutted and

[8] p. 295.

raped by the non-European world. And in the efficiency and ruthlessness of their exploitation these new or newly-awakened societies have rapidly surpassed their masters: the vast spaces at their command and the passive, plastic character of their populations have permitted them all sorts of short-cuts. Thus they have been able to turn the arts of Europe against the original inventors—and the final paradox of the matter is that the victim (as in the myth) has consented to her own disgrace through loss of nerve and senseless self-division.

Such is the theme that *The Rape of Europe* pursues through a fascinating series of chapters on city and countryside, the secularization of religion, alienation in art, nation and supernation, and Europe as the "sorcerer's apprentice" of modern technology. Sometimes pretentious, frequently wordy, each chapter offers enough in the way of originality and illumination to make it worth reading. Indeed the whole book deserves careful attention providing it is read in the proper way—not as history in the strict sense but as variations on a theme, a pastiche of a Bach fugue, which its author, in company with Spengler, regards as the "supreme gospel of Europe's supreme art." [9]

*   *   *

The stout volume of *Reconsiderations* (New York, 1961) which Toynbee has appended to his already imposing *Study of History* will surely take rank as one of the strangest literary endeavors of our time. In it the author of a scholarly enterprise that has occupied his entire mature life—nearly half a century—has tried to reckon with all the dozens of critics, great and small, who have been nibbling away at his monument since 1934, when the first set of volumes was published. Simply to understand and digest such masses of disagreement, much of it obtuse and vituperative, would have been enough for an ordinary historian. But Toynbee has never thought of himself as an ordinary historian— hence the fury of his critics—and for him nothing would do but

[9] p. 234.

laboriously, painstakingly, masochistically to refute or to accept
every last charge levelled against him.

The reckoning falls under two main heads. The first in-
volves concessions of substance—modifications in his structure of
comparative history that Toynbee has made under the pressure of
his critics or his own advances in thought and knowledge. He has
altered his presentation of several early civilizations to take account of recent archaeological discoveries; in particular he has
reconsidered his view of Jewish history, half-apologizing for his
use of the term "fossil" (which had grieved a number of Judaic
scholars) and broadening his treatment to include a considera-
tion of the *diaspora* as a phenomenon common to many different
societies. He has simplified (and, I think, greatly improved) his
listing of comparable civilizations, and in so doing he has confessed that his "model" for the cycle of growth and disintegration
in these cultures was too exclusively Hellenic in origin and that it
needed to be combined with another model drawn from the history of China. Finally, and most significantly, he has decided that
the "higher religions" should no longer be "assigned . . . to this
or that civilization" as its "religious component." "Religion," he
writes, "cannot be called to heel, like a dog, to suit human con-
venience." [10] It must be given its own higher standing-ground,
outside and above the ordinary course of human affairs.

The second area of concession to criticism is more philosophical. The fundamental point, Toynbee finds, that has been
contested in his work has been his claim to an empirical method
of inquiry: his critics have accused him of trying "to force the
phenomena" of history into an "arbitrary framework at the cost
of distorting the truth." [11] Here Toynbee, to my mind, quite puts
his detractors to rout. With examples drawn from a wide range
of scientific and humanistic studies, he drives home the argument that *all* systematic presentation of material has a certain
quality of arbitrariness and of personal intellectual construction:

[10] pp. 89, 95.
[11] p. 3.

the human mind can work in no other fashion. And beyond the range of verified historical knowledge, myth and fantasy necessarily take over. What he has offered us, Toynbee explains, is not *the* truth about history; it is simply the way one Englishman born in 1889 has happened to see it.

All this is excellent and conforms to the most advanced contemporary definitions of scientific and historical method. But it is not what Toynbee originally set out to do. At the start and in his earlier volumes, his attitude toward his work was more positivist and self-assured: he was telling us that history actually had a structure and that he personally had discovered it. One reason he was so confident was that he knew very little of contemporary social science and scientific method; his education, he . confesses, had been narrowly classical, and when he began his study he knew almost nothing of Freud and Weber and Durkheim and the other twentieth-century masters of thought about human society. Nor could he know the word "model," which has come into general use only in the last generation. Now, after the belated discovery of this as of so much else that might have helped him at the start, he assures us that all along he was presenting no more than one of the many possible "models" for the comparative study of civilizations.

Yet this chastened and sophisticated Toynbee finds it difficult to maintain with any consistency his new subjectivist stand. He is constantly relapsing into his old positivist phraseology and biological metaphors. And understandably so—for he is too old a dog to master such modish intellectual tricks. If he had *really* changed that much, he would have had to ask himself whether he should have embarked on his life's work at all, or rather, whether he should not have cast it in quite a different form, as a series of essays or suggestions, instead of a monumental work which purported to give a tight explanation for the whole course of human history.

This is where the area of substantive criticism joins the one of method and philosophy. In the present volume Toynbee for the first time makes explicit a change in his own outlook which was beginning to be apparent in volumes 4–6 and which clearly emerged in volumes 7–10, published in 1954. The work has ceased to be a study of the life cycles of comparable civilizations —the task which Spengler was the first to carry out, and with a power of thought and imagery which Toynbee has never equalled; it has become, rather, the history of man's upward progress through the agency of the higher religions. It has ceased to be—if it ever was—either social science or historical literature in the usual meaning of the terms; it has become a history of salvation.

In 1952—before the later volumes of *A Study of History* were published—I observed in the original edition of this book that Toynbee was more of a poet and "intuitive seer" than he realized and that his religious faith kept getting in the way of his comparative study of human societies. In his *Reconsiderations,* Toynbee quotes these remarks, but without refuting or accepting them, as he has done with most of the criticisms directed against his work. I interpret this to mean either that Toynbee finds my arguments unanswerable or that he agrees with me and cannot bring himself to say so, since to do so would be to call in question the very nature of his life's enterprise. It is significant, I think, that he now emphasizes the work of a precursor—Giambattista Vico—who did not figure prominently in his earlier volumes, a writer of a genius similar to his own, who jumbled together mythology and would-be science, and who, as Toynbee himself notes, "was pulled in contrary directions by his critical faculty and by his Christian convictions." [12]

If this is true, then most of the controversy between Toynbee and his critics has been quite beside the point—a dialogue of the deaf and dumb. Toynbee seems to be conceding a great deal, but he has in fact relinquished very little of his fundamental standing ground. Psychiatry is familiar with "overcompliance" as a particularly insidious form of resistance; Toynbee's professions of modesty and doubt have always been ineffective in cloaking his cosmic intellectual ambitions. True, he has abandoned his

[12] pp. 5, 653.

pretension to a positivist charting of a single pattern for human history—but this was a mistaken idea from the start, and it was only Toynbee's lack of intellectual preparation for his task that made him take so long to see that it was not what he was after. Beyond this concession—which actually cost him nothing, since philosophical positivism was temperamentally uncongenial to him—he has refused to do what the vast majority of his critics have demanded, that is, to convert himself into a conventional historian. There are only a few of us who have asked of him nothing more than to appear under his true colors—in the guise for which his classical education admirably equipped him—as Vico's successor in the imaginative manipulation of myth and poetry for the understanding of man's past. This he has almost done in his present volume: the only thing that has held him back from a relativist recognition of his place in the history of human thought has been his groping quest for religious faith.

Hence I for one am sorry that Toynbee has felt obliged to recite *mea culpa* so thoroughly. I regret that he has blurred the clear image of his work that emerged from his earlier volumes. I wager that a generation from now people will take his first ten volumes straight—or, more likely, the two-volume Somervell abridgement of them—without paying much attention to his *Reconsiderations*. Toynbee's *Study of History* is a monument that deserves to stand unaltered—a great work with glaring faults (for such are the occupational hazards of writing great works). This last volume is to be read primarily for its psychological interest, as a different type of monument to an honest mind, only half conscious of its own motivations, at grips with the hopeless task of being fair to all parties in one of the major intellectual controversies of our era.[13]

[13] Portions of this appendix were earlier published in *The American Historical Review* and the *New York Herald-Tribune Books*.

INDEX